Do you work here?
The shop floor chronicles

Michael Ethelson

Retail therapy: Psychiatric assistance that should be offered to anyone working on the shop floor.

DEDICATION

To all and anyone, past, present, and future, who have found themselves working on the very unique frontline that is the shop floor. You are heroes in your own right, and people need to acknowledge the fact.

And to my best friend Jack.
Border Terrier, pub buddy and devourer of pork scratchings. Missed but never forgotten.
"Your lead is still on its hook lad."

ACKNOWLEDGMENTS

To all of you, you know who you are, that have helped me on my journey from what was just an initial idea to an actual book.

And to those of you who have no idea that your antics have now been immortalised.

INTRODUCTION

"Do you work here?"

Looking down at my grocer's apron and specifically at the large blue letters on the left of my chest, I felt pretty confident, as I pointed at said letters and answered. "Yes madam, I do work here."

The idea of chronicling the experiences of someone working in grocery retail on the shop floor is not an obvious attention grabber. So, it is great that you have come this far.

If you have ever worked in retail, or indeed still do, (particularly grocery retail) then most of what you are about to read is probably not a revelation at all. The characters and the situations you find yourself in, having to navigate around people's behaviours, day in day out, are probably commonplace.

Much of what is being shared with you is based upon, and inspired by, real life experiences, actual events and observations made during a brief, but eye-opening, episode into the world of grocery retail, by the author. Specifically on the shop floor. With additional material and insight being provided by several others. Namely close friends, family, and fellow shop floor workers, all of whom collectively have decades of experience and stories to share. Most of which has been weaved into the storylines of this book.

Do you work here? – The shop floor chronicles - is based within The Country Produce Store. A fictional location providing a very real nonfiction shop floor insight. Where reality and the surreal often clash to provide a sometimes amusing, often outrageous look inside the world of the shop floor worker.

Following Michael on his brief voyage of retail discovery. We begin with his wife floating the questionable notion of him working at the shop, his subsequent surreal interview, the surprisingly novel induction and into a world like no other. The mayhem that is Christmas and how the season of goodwill is anything but. A glimpse into the madness that is panic buying, and the morons who do it. And the helplessness of being a bystander to the scourge that is shoplifting. And everything in between.

Featuring, of course, the real protagonists, the true backbone of the shop. An eclectic mix of people that formed what was an effective, but often dysfunctional team. Endeavouring to make the place perfect at the beginning of the day and putting it all back together at the end once the customers had left the building.

And finally, not forgetting those unique

personalities that are the customers. Some great, some not so. But equally as real. The belligerents, the coffee morning mums and the entitled sorts, to name but a few. Those that decided, at some point in their lives, that good manners and social graces are not for them. But then there are the good guys. The people who, often unwittingly, make the shop floor workers day a delight. So, a huge and sincere thanks is offered to all those customers because without your appalling and wonderful behaviours this book would have little or no content. That being said, this book is not about customer bashing. If anything, it's about raising an awareness of the plight of thousands of shop floor workers and typically what they must contend with every day.

There's a book, which you may have read, written by a young doctor. Where he shares his experiences of working on the frontline within the National Health Service (NHS). The many anecdotes and stories provide the reader with a humorous look into what is clearly one of the most challenging working environments anywhere. However, behind the humour there was insight. Insight into how poorly many of the public treat people in service. People who want nothing more than to go to work each day, with no agenda other than to help those in need.

Whilst few, if any, life-or-death decisions are made by those working on the frontline within grocery retail, let's take a minute to reflect on the fact that they also go to work each day, with no agenda, other than to ensure that the shop floor is fit for purpose, and satisfies that most basic of needs. For the general public (you and me) to be able to buy essential things for life: such as food for example. None of which happens by accident, but by a huge amount of effort and commitment on the part of those often-invisible foot soldiers: the shop floor workers.

Like our author doctor, much of the following is presented in the form of humour. But behind the humour there are numerous messages: some subtle, some not so. I hope you enjoy the humour, and for those of you that do not work, or have never worked, in retail: Please grasp the messages.

ONE

MICHAEL LEARNS THAT THE ONE SURE THING IN LIFE
IS THAT THERE ARE NO SURE THINGS.

Lights, (CCTV) cameras, action!

I have cash in my till and I'm ready to go. "And who's ready to checkout? Next please!" as I look up endeavouring, as always, to try and inject some humour into the small line of customers waiting at a respectful distance from the only till in operation at this early time of the day – mine.

I should have known better, of course, having noticed that one or two of those in the queue were regulars to The Country Produce Store and of an age where 'checking out' could become a permanent state anytime soon.

But first up was a young girl, with, who I assumed to be, her mum and dad. None of whom looked particularly happy with life, especially the little girl who I'm guessing was about five or six years old.

You will have to forgive me for not being more precise, but I'm of an age where I usually tend to gauge the age of children by their height and size – including my own who I now simply classify as young adults, thus avoiding the need to remember their actual ages. Other classifications are babies, the ones that need to be carried; toddlers, those that don't, small children who are often chatty and quite inquisitive, and older children who have no need for human engagement whatsoever, other than with their smartphones.

With eyes that had clearly been crying lately and the father, noticing my concern, announced that his daughter was sad because she'd lost her kitten recently. I looked at the little girl with what I hoped to be a look of compassion. Whereupon she confirmed as much with a slight nod of the head. If you knew my face, you'd know that I am capable of just two looks, blank and less blank, having adopted the skill of customer proofing my face some while ago. Although I was once told by a customer, a fellow with a lazy eye, that I do have an engaging smile. I thanked him for the compliment despite my colleague insisting that he was looking at her at the time.

Unlike dogs who at least give an impression of being your friend, especially at mealtimes, cats to my mind are just freeloaders. They come and go as they please, they won't think twice before scratching your hand because you dared to stroke them at an inconvenient time, and they kill birds – for no particular reason other than because they can. So, any sympathy I had wasn't for the small cat but for the little girl. But customers imparting their bad news isn't an unusual occurrence, especially when you're working at the checkout. As such, I learnt right at the very beginning of my tenure at The County Produce Store never to ask a customer, "How are you today?" Reason being is that many of them, especially the older sorts, are inclined to want to tell you, sometimes in extraordinary detail, about their numerous ailments. Don't get me wrong, it's not that I'm an uncaring soul, I'm just not interested.

However, on this occasion I saw an opportunity to help a little girl in her hour of sorrow. So, turning to dad and with the most encouraging smile I could muster announced that, "I have an idea!"

I've seen confused on a face many times before in my life, often as a result of me saying something. But the look on this occasion was more than that, it was almost pleading for me to stop talking. "I don't understand, how is it that you think you can help? I mean if you somehow have a kitten tucked up your sleeve then sorry no we're not interested, but thanks anyway." Now just glaring at me and at the same time challenging me not to say another word.

Genuinely confused, and slightly miffed by his attitude I took up the challenge and continued. "No, I don't have another kitten up my sleeve, sir. What I'm suggesting is that we can maybe help your daughter get her cat back by putting a notice up on the public noticeboard by the entrance. And if you have a photo then that would be great. 'Have you seen this kitten, please phone this number…' that type of thing, what do you think?"

Out of the corner of my eye I could see that for some reason his wife was looking horrified at my suggestion. But the little girl's face lit up with a huge smile. That was enough for me and in that moment, I felt pretty good about myself. Until that is her dad took me to one side, out of earshot of anyone else, least of all his wife and daughter, and whispered, "Not lost you numbskull, but lost in the dead sense. It got run over and is now in a hole, at the bottom of our garden, marked with a cross made from an ice-lolly stick. So good luck with the card in the window thing, mate." Leaving me with nothing more to say other than, "Are you paying with cash or card today, sir?" Mum and dad took their shopping and, without looking back, made for the exit with the little girl tugging at her dad's sleeve excitedly telling him how I was going to get Dave back from the angels for her.

And that was it. Yet another, but hardly unusual, episode in this shitty, wonderful job on the shop floor.

There are many reasons why a retiree, such as me, might consider going back into the workplace, such as: Economical, boredom, mental health, can't stand being in the same room as their partner, rubbish at golf or perhaps in denial of how old they really are. Six months previous I had never considered a job in retail. In fact, I'd never considered going back to work at all. To some, at fifty-eight, I had taken early retirement. To me I'd simply had enough of IT and working on our two-hundred-year-old money pit of a house seemed like the perfect hiding place.

We live in a designated AONB (Area of

Outstanding Natural Beauty), or as our son puts it, Area of Old Narky Bastards – otherwise referred to as the walking dead. A place where cream teas meet Jurassic fossils - many of whom frequent The Country Produce Store – in what we reckoned to be our 'forever' home. Although with us having moved house nine times in thirty-two years, with the last two also allegedly being our 'forever' homes you'll have to excuse my scepticism. The truth is my knees, back and pretty much all the other moving parts of my body are telling me that it really ought to be our final project.

As it turned out, I was to be handed a break from my hard labour, albeit a forced one.

TWO

THE PLAN FOR MICHAEL'S FUTURE HAS BEEN
DETERMINED. HIS WIFE IS EQUALLY DETERMINED
THAT THE PLAN BECOMES A REALITY.

"Work on the house is coming to a bit of a stop, for a year at least I reckon." I announced to Elaine, my wife, as we were just finishing up in the garden, having completed some midwinter ongoing repairs to the fence.

"What do you mean?" Elaine replied. Not in an accusatory tone mind you but very close.

"Well, the planning application for the upstairs bathroom looks like it could take a few months, and we haven't even had a visit from the Conservation Nazis yet." She of course knew who I was referring to, as we'd been through planning in a conservation area some years before. On that occasion a whole minibus full of high vis geriatrics turned up, each with a clipboard and a variety of walking aids. We knew the visit was on the cards, it was just the number and age of the people that took us by surprise. It was then that we realised that the pork scratchings and lager we'd got in especially to somehow loosen the morals of the planners would be to no avail. And despite our need at the time to get our plans approved we drew the line at chewing the food for our esteemed guests, so as to avoid a denture catastrophe on their part.

"Maybe I should have baked a Victoria sponge." Elaine reflected as we watched the group being helped down the single step of the minibus by the driver. During their brief visit none of the group acknowledged our existence as they strode purposefully through the garden, ignoring the proposed building plot, heading instead, and nodding sagely, to the in-bloom wisteria that covered the back of our then cottage. Some months later permission was granted to demolish the outside toilet. Or 'Infestation House' as we called it, due to the number of rats that seemed to find the place a cozy retreat where they could endlessly piss and procreate.

Of course, my announcement of our current application came as no surprise to Elaine because she was as frustrated with the whole planning business as I was. Also, having promised to avoid listed buildings and conservation areas after the last debacle, how is it, we found ourselves in the same situation? I'll tell you how, it's because we have a particular soft spot for old houses, especially those considered by romantics as 'chocolate box' cottages. And ours was very old and, at the time we bought it, really run down. To the point where most of the roof was on the ground. But here's the thing with listed properties in England, whether in or outside of conservation areas: nobody in the local conservation department has any interest in them, until that is someone comes along and buys it with a view to bringing it back to its former glory. Then these, previously invisible, people are all over it, having an opinion on all and any works you intend to do on the place.

But the thing that did surprise me was how quickly Elaine came up with a solution for my continued employment. "Have you thought about working at the shop?" She did a few days a week working on the delicatessen in The Country Produce Store, so I knew this to be what she meant by "the shop".

"No, but you clearly have!" Amazing how, when you get old, not only is there a heightened interest from complete strangers in your prostate, but also from your family regarding how any spare time you might have can be filled.

Situated just a few miles down the road from our house, on the perimeter of what used to be a sizable dairy farm, The Country Produce Store opened in the early noughties and was the brainchild of the then dairy farmer and his wife, locally known simply as the farmer and his wife. The nineteenth century stone and thatch barn, with vaulted oak interior became the first iteration of what is now known as The Country Produce Store. Originally, and still referred to by many, as simply the 'Farm Shop'. Since those early days it has undergone considerable updating and been greatly extended, though not necessarily sympathetically. It could be one of any number of the farm shops dotted around our country, most of which I am sure started out with the idealistic dream and sound principles of wanting to bring freshly farmed and locally produced food directly to the masses. 'field to fork', that type of thing. In other words, removing the need for the business to have any affiliation with large national or international food producers, supermarket chains or other third parties.

I'm assured that quite a few still do adhere to those principles and are very successful businesses within their own right. However, over time (either by design, necessity, or chance) many, including The Country Produce Store, have turned to attracting, not so much the masses, but a more exclusive or, as someone once told me, the more 'discerning' shopper. I was to subsequently learn that a discerning shopper is more of a reference to the 'well-heeled' sorts. Or, as our son insists, 'the old narky bastards.' During my time on the shop floor, I found this particular environment to be an incubator for the type of people that find it necessary (and easy) to be anything other than civil. And as much as you may have heard it said that the "customer is always right", I can assure you, that whilst in some universe or other that may be the case, you should know that the customer is not always 'correct'.

Being correct = *Well mannered, reasonable, civil, polite, attentive, accepting, observant, understanding, patient, agreeable, interested, and empathetic.*

But I'm getting ahead of myself, as I'll tell you more about these people, and multiple others a bit later.

And so it was, over a cup of tea, that Elaine told me more about what The Country Produce Store was looking for. Simply put, they were looking for people to work on the shop floor. Going on to tell me that there was a particular and immediate need, as some bloke or other was due to leave at the end of the month. Slightly puzzled I asked, "But what has any of that got to do with me and our delayed planning application?"

Continuing as if I hadn't spoken, she added, "Personally I think you'd be great. Think of it as another adventure." For some reason or other she felt that I would be more than qualified to fill this immediate need, and now that I had time on my hands, she reckoned I could do maybe two or three days a week. And endeavouring to put a positive spin on this preposterous idea, telling me that in doing so we'd get to see a lot more of one another. My wife is a remarkable woman, so she tells me, particularly when it comes to anticipating and knowing what's good for me. Even before I do.

"I'm in favour of adventure, but I'd prefer to have some say in what that adventure looks like. I'm pretty sure that Captain Scott didn't rely on his wife to plan his adventures for him." Crossing my arms in the belief that I was giving the point more emphasis, when in actual fact I was making no more of an impact than a spoilt child might.

"You're right about Captain Scott, but then look

how he ended up."

I needed to head this off at the pass because, unbeknown to her, I'd already had some thoughts of my own – I know hard to believe eh? – and not one of those included working in a shop, least of all The Country Produce Store. In desperation I reminded her of the fact that despite her flattering reference to the contrary I had no previous retail experience, adding, that as an old IT person for thirty-five plus years I was genuinely struggling to see any obvious synergy, between my skills and that of a shop floor person.

In addition to being remarkable, my wife also has dogged perseverance, especially when she gets a bee in her bonnet about something. And this idea of me working in the shop was one such bee. As much as I threw up what - in hindsight - amounted to pathetic objections, she was able to fire back a positive contradiction each time.

"I really don't know why you're being so difficult about this Michael. It's just an idea." Which of course it wasn't. It was already baked and ready to be served up. And the fact that she called me 'Michael' and not 'Mike' didn't go unnoticed either. She is both good cop and bad cop rolled into one. She continued, "And despite the fact that you don't have many friends, you're actually quite good with people. I'd even go as far as to say that you can be quite personable when you put your mind to it." See what I mean good cop, bad cop, as I was left struggling to pick out the compliments from the barbs.

Though she wasn't done yet. "You also enjoy a bit of banter; just look how you are in the pub."

"But my banter is often fuelled by lager and unless you tell me otherwise, I'm guessing that being drunk on the shop floor, although probably necessary, isn't generally allowed."

She just looked at me and shook her head in a way that suggested I was now verging on the pathetic. And if the truth were told she was right. Quickly running out of contrary arguments, I came to accept that for my own domestic health I should at least consider the idea. Plus, in doing so, I could buy myself some time to come up with a more convincing line of defence as to why this really wasn't such a good idea.

The problem I was having is that being spontaneous isn't a natural characteristic of an IT guy. With any computer challenge I would have had to think long and hard, often consulting with some third party or other, before arriving at a solution. I have been known to cogitate for hours before finally deciding to 'switch it (the computer) off and then back on again'. But over the years I had learnt that there was no switching Elaine off. Her stamina is legendary in our house, and she had no intention of letting the subject drop. Any thoughts of buying myself time quickly evaporated when she got up from the table and announced, "I'm going to give Gavin the store manager a ring. It would be great if he's got some time to see you today – wouldn't it?" With the last bit said with just the right amount of venom daring me to disagree. "Yes, that would be wonderful." Said with as much enthusiasm as I could muster, like someone who was being forcibly dragged in to see the headmaster. Even the thought of having passed some kind of 'fit for purpose test' gave me little comfort. Much like passing the 'fit for purpose test' to be sent to a penal colony.

I never realised how much the thought of me relaxing and doing nothing much had been troubling my wife.

Falling back on that very pitiful high ground of nothing ventured, nothing gained, I conceded the debate and agreed to her making the call. And went to say as much, as she put her finger to her lips in a 'stop talking' motion because she'd already gotten through to the shop switchboard – the managers wife.

At least I couldn't be blamed for not giving it a shot – pathetic I know. But then in my own mind (like I have one of my own) in allowing this to continue I was still leaving a more agreeable door slightly ajar, to pursue something more satisfying for the next year or so. Such as becoming a local beer critic perhaps. After all, what qualifications do you really need to be any kind of critic? Especially when it comes to food and drink.

I'm pretty sure I'm capable of surreptitiously visiting a few pubs and tasting whatever beers are on offer and then, under a pseudonym, writing a review or two. Then post them in the Furrowed Brows magazine (our local freebee magazine) or on social media. After a few five-star reviews I would reveal my true identity and live out my days, or at least until planning permission is granted, on free hospitality.

Seemed like the perfect plan to me, but first there was the looming prospect of The Country Produce Store to deal with. And in that moment, I wasn't dealing with it too well.

Slightly over enthusiastically, in my opinion, Elaine came back into the kitchen and announced, "well I spoke with Gavin, and he does have some time this afternoon if you wanted to pop in and see him."

Really? Did she just say "…if you wanted to pop in and see him." Ha ha! I love it that she's giving me a choice. Leaving me to wonder how she would react if I were to say, *"actually, no I don't want to pop in and see him."* But immediately thought better of it and instead readily (but not so enthusiastically) agreed to go see him.

In order to maintain the notion that I was taking her idea seriously, I set about printing down my CV. Something that hadn't seen the light of day for a few years. "Do you think I ought to include my recent work experience?"

"Such as? You haven't had any recent work experience."

"How dare you! What about the work I've been doing on this money-pit of a house? Then there's the bins. They don't get put out on their own you know. And then there's cleaning your car, and repairing that excuse for a fence, which by the way, isn't even ours it's that lazy twats' next door?" I have no idea why I was getting so het up, but I did. Elaine on the other hand remained cool and simply said "No." And then quietly left the room for me to reflect on my behaviour, once again as a child might.

So, armed with my wholly unsuitable CV, showing off my glorious thirty plus years in IT, I set off for my interview. Which incidentally was also something I hadn't done for years. But let me tell you that one of my most notable abilities is to excel at interviews. My starting point is that it's not up to me to match their requirements with the right candidate. That is most definitely the employer's job. On one occasion in my response to a 'no thank you letter' I told them that despite them wasting my time there were no hard feelings, but they needed to do better next time.

Call it conditioning, call it what you like, but as much as I was a reluctant candidate, I considered that an interview is an interview. Meaning that it needed to be taken seriously and first impressions count. So, I decided to tidy myself up a bit. Not to the point of wearing a suit, (because I no longer owned a suit) but a clean shirt, smart(ish) pair of trousers: that type of thing. I even cleaned the one pair of decent boots I still own.

Elaine insisted on driving me there, either to avoid me getting lost and ending up in the pub I assumed. Upon arrival she introduced me to Gavin, stopping short of asking me if I had my dinner money and to be a good boy for the nice man.

Michael Ethelson

THREE

AN UNQUALIFIED BUT SUITABLY QUALIFIED MAN
ATTENDS AN INTERVIEW.

"Hi, I'm Michael and thanks for seeing me at such short notice." offering my hand, but Gavin had other ideas and simply smiled and directed me into the building.

I'd been to the shop on numerous occasions, but this was my first time behind the scenes so to speak, as I found myself in the stockroom. We eventually shook hands, and I was shown into what I took to be a small meeting room resplendent with an old oak dining table and an array of odd chairs.

"Welcome young Michael, we've been expecting you for some time now. Would you like a hot drink?" Delivered, for some reason, in the way of some Bond villain or other.

The other thing was that Gavin must have been at least twenty years my junior, but I nonetheless decided to play along. "Is that right old man, well I'm pleased to have made it safely and apologies for the delay in getting here. And yes please, I'd love a coffee." I guess I could have added, "shaken but not stirred," but there's a thin line between playing along and being downright daft.

Shouting back down the corridor to no one in particular, in an authoritative voice that he was clearly not used to using, "two coffees please!" and then sweeping an arm around the room Gavin delighted in telling me, "So this Michael is where all the big decisions are made."

Taking in the dust around the place. "So I'm guessing nothing groundbreaking has happened for a while then?" At which point the room fell into silence.

Two of the four walls were adorned with numerous poster sized photographs showing different species of livestock, which I thought was very in keeping with this being a farm shop and all. Although the picture of Kenny Dalglish, 1970's Scottish and Liverpool footballer, did seem out of place, but I decided to overlook it. All the pictures were faded, having clearly been on the wall for many years, including a heavily framed piece of embroidery stitched into words that I took to be the company motto:

WELCOME TO THE FUNNY FARM

With Gavin looking around the room as if it was his first time too, I had the chance to take in this captain of the funny farm. He was of small build or small boned as my gran would have said, short in stature, unnaturally smooth white skin for a bloke, as though puberty had passed him by. And strangely round when his frame said he should be anything but. There were no sharp corners to speak of and no ledges on his head for his spectacles to cling on to. So, he was constantly pushing them back towards his face with his forefinger. Beige trousers only accentuated his nondescript nature, as did his short sleeved white shirt, clearly made for a much smaller person.

I held this morbid fascination for just a few seconds more as I came to realise that he seemed a bit on edge. Maybe my power dressing intimidated him? So, to break the ice I pointed up to the wall at the livestock posters and Kenny Dalglish, and asked, "Family?"

Looking at the pictures, squinting a little, as if he'd only just noticed them. "No, those are some of the prize-winning animals once owned by The Country Produce Store owners long before my time. They're long gone now, as indeed is the farmer and his wife who, I don't know if you know, started this enterprise." All relayed to me impassively as his initial enthusiasm at meeting me seemed to have just drained away.

Trying to keep some kind of momentum going and deciding against enquiring after Kenny Dalglish, I offered back, "What, for breeding purposes? I'm sure I read somewhere that the sperm of some high-end bulls is quite valuable, not sure about pigs though."

Do you work here? – The shop floor chronicles

"No, I think that most of the pigs ended up in our award-winning sausages. Although we haven't won an award for a while now. My boss and shop owner, Gareth, doesn't hold much store in awards. Not sure about the others. I can find out for you if you're interested." Keeping up with his monotone demeanour.

Without being asked I sat down on one of the odd chairs and Gavin did the same, but opposite me. "No, you're alright, I was just trying to ease us into the meeting to be honest." At which point he visibly relaxed.

With the ice broken, I proceeded to tell him about my background: thirty years, IT, Exec... yardy yardy ya. In other words, how ill-equipped I was for a life in retail. Going on to explain that I had no practical knowledge of the shop floor, although my previous customer facing experience could, at a push, perhaps be put to good use in the shop. I needed to strike a balance between being serious about the interview and not really having any interest at all in working at The Country Produce Store. This meant that when I reported back to the command centre, I could, with some conscience have a credible story that says "I did my best love, but despite everything it turns out that I really wasn't qualified for the job after all. C'est la vie."

Having only been in the room for what I reckoned to be less than ten minutes we kind of dried up. With no questions coming back my way we fell into an easy silence. I looked up at the clock, that had stopped long ago, and was now permanently stuck on seven minutes past eight. Much like this interview.

To be honest, at that moment, I'd probably had more balanced conversations with my dog than I was having with Gavin.

But I needed to string this out a bit longer, otherwise Elaine would see right through my ruse. As a result, I went on to ask Gavin some general questions about retail and his time in the sector. At which point he became really animated, energised, almost overly enthusiastic about the whole subject. Taking me on a journey through all his years of experience in grocery retail. Where he started on the shop floor in a small shop, then going on to work for a high-end supermarket for over 10 years, rising to become a deputy assistant section manager, or something – I can't remember. And how he couldn't imagine doing anything else having lived by the mantra; "The customer is always right," as though he himself was the author of this, in my opinion, very dubious statement, and not a couple of truly successful retailers over a hundred years ago.

This outpouring seemed to almost exhaust him as he pushed his spectacles back towards his face and settled back into silence, gazing out of the window, as if in a dream.

The room is quiet once more, and I'm left thinking that maybe his spectacles are solar panels, and he was on a recharge cycle? But nonetheless it gave me some time to reflect on what he had said. Until that moment I had never considered grocery retail to be 'a calling'. I had always thought of it as just a job. But Gavin's passion was living proof that to some people it clearly is a lot more.

He came out of his reverie – partially recharged – and, realising I was still in the room. "Tell me, what do you think of Dunstone Town's chances of avoiding relegation this year?"

Elaine had spoken about this little foible of his on a few occasions, where he was known for asking people random questions but not hanging around long enough for an answer. She put it down to nerves or perhaps the need to maybe break an awkward silence. Or indeed that strange obligation many people suffer with, where they have to say something, anything, at the point of passing in a corridor. As he was approaching her in the back corridor of the shop one morning he said, "I've heard that Malta is a nice place to live, what do you reckon?" And then walked on without waiting for a response. On another occasion, this time breezing past the delicatessen, he announced, "Good morning, Elaine, lovely day, we had a really lovely fish pie last night. Do you like fish pie?" Once again walking on without waiting for a reply.

Back in the room. "I'm sorry but I have no real idea who Dunstone Town are. Are they a rugby team or football team?"

"No, they're a hockey team based up north." And with that he went back into recharge mode. This was getting really bizarre and even more so when he went on to ask, "So, what are your thoughts on the new Skoda SUV?"

At this point I decided that I needed to plan my escape, but he had the door covered and the windows looked like they hadn't been open for years. Then the penny dropped. Maybe this wasn't just some madman asking me random questions after all: It was all part of the interview process. One of those behavioural interview techniques gauging how I would react when faced with the unexpected. After all, he had previously worked for a high-end supermarket so maybe they use these types of techniques to ensure that they get the best of the best people? Problem is if this was indeed the case then he was wasting his time because I was probably the worst of the worst insofar as having someone like me working on his shop floor.

So decided to say as much. "Alright I get it. Those dumb questions were really a test, right?" Which immediately made him sit up. But he wasn't smiling, in fact he looked really offended. "I'm sorry, I don't know what you mean!"

"You know the trick questions about Dunstone something or other and the Skoda thing, it was a test right, to see how I'd react?"

As it turned out it was none of those things. Gavin really did want to know my views on the Skoda as he was thinking of buying one, and his son had just started playing for Dunstone.

Time to change the subject and bring us back to earth. "So, can you tell me some more about the place Gavin, your role, what can I look forward to if I'm successful in this interview?"

And with that the animated and energised Gavin came back into the room. "Well I've been here for three years now and in that time, under my leadership, the place has really changed. My being here has turned us into the dynamic business you see today. You'd be surprised how much there is to this business, the different facets, its multiple dimensions. To the unwitting outsider it might seem like any old farm shop. But it's not, I can assure you. I'd like to think that my management team look upon me as not only their leader, but as a bit of a juggler - without any balls, obviously. And we're quite a forward thinking shop you know."

"How so?" Trying desperately to sound interested.

"Well for example we've moved away from plastic bags and now provide paper bags for our customers to put their fruit and vegetables in."

"Like they used to in the nineteen fifties you mean?" I was tempted to ask whether he had considered closing the shop on a Wednesday afternoon and all-day Sunday, as they also used to in the old days, but thought better of it.

And with that a look of triumph settled across his face, having delivered what he clearly thought was an impressive monologue. Almost exhausted, though clearly feeling the need to ask me a question, he turned his head ninety degrees, endeavouring it seemed, to look me in the eye. "So tell me about your thoughts on the place Michael. And why do you want to work here?"

"Well Gavin, it certainly doesn't seem like any old farm shop, and I can see exactly why your management team might consider you as their ball-less juggler. Oh, and the customer is always right, of course." In the absence of anything original I find it best to always quote the other person's words back to them. And if you can't think of a suitable answer then ignore the question altogether, which is why I chose to ignore his second question about why I wanted to work there.

Anyway, long story short, it seemed as though the shop really were desperate. Because despite my best efforts at trying *not* to get the job and my lack of retail experience, I was offered a zero hours contract for a position on the shop floor.

Or maybe I'm being hard on myself, and in the fifteen minutes or so that we'd spent together Gavin saw something in me that he could fashion and mould to become a prize asset for The Country Produce Store. In time there may well be a framed poster of me in the meeting room for future employees to gaze upon in admiration. My sperm may even be... Sorry I'm getting carried away now.

So exactly what did a zero hours contract mean to me? Well, when called upon I would be expected to work a 10-hour shift (except Sunday which would be an 8-hour shift) and all for the (not so) generous hourly rate of less than the recommended living wage. In short, this meant that if all went well I would be working for two or three days a week and every other weekend. And at the end of the month my take home pay would be pretty much what I used to earn in a day and a half in my IT days. Oh, and should one or other of us decide that this arrangement wasn't working, or we just don't like one another, we can just shake hands and part company with immediate effect. Although in time I was to learn two things regarding my employment. Firstly, and as I've already mentioned, they were desperate. And second it would be almost impossible to get the sack from The Country Produce Store. Short of buggering Gavin that is. So, no chance at all then.

As for my wife, it would no doubt be mission accomplished. A short-term gap in my life would be filled, hopefully with something that she insisted I would enjoy. And the only way I was going to find that out was to push on. The Country Produce Store would get nothing less than my best.

So not a distinguished beer critic after all, but a shop floor worker.

* * *

Not giving me any opportunity to change my mind Gavin took my hand, shook it rigorously in a "welcome to the family" kind of way and in doing so, I couldn't help noticing the relief on his face. Anyway, with his other hand in the small of my back, I was led out of the meeting room and along the short corridor to meet my day-to-day boss: the shop floor manager.

I was also introduced to one or two others, most of whose names I instantly forgot. Don't get me wrong I'm not a particularly rude person it just seems to be a me thing. You can introduce me to any number of people and within minutes I've forgotten their names.

Over the years I've tried all sorts of aide memoires, but to no avail. I remember one such tip being to think of an object or an animal that sounded like or rhymed with the person's name. So, when I see them again, a picture of that animal or object would form in my mind, which in turn would connect to their name. Having travelled extensively in my job I met quite a few people, many of whom didn't have easy to pronounce nor easy to remember names. Even those that did, I was still useless. On one occasion I remember being introduced to the European CEO of a large tech company, a French lady called Madame Blondin (pronounced Blanda). Putting my newly discovered memory aid into action, I thought of Blanda as sounding like Blondie, as in the 1970's pop group fronted by the extremely talented Debbie Harry. So, for the remainder of the evening, I proudly, and confidently I might add, introduced my colleagues (and quite a few others) to Madam Arry, remembering of course how the French like to drop their H's.

I'm pleased to report that I did, overtime, get to grips with the names of everyone that I both worked with and for in The Country Produce Store. The shop floor manager, who I mentioned previously, was a lady by the name of Angela made two immediate impressions on me. The first being that she seemed genuinely delighted that I had agreed to work there; the other being that she didn't really want to be there.

Gavin made the introductions. "Angela, this is Michael, he's going to be working for us. Or rather he's going to be working for *you*. And he's available immediately." I didn't seem to recall us discussing my availability, but before I could challenge the point, he was already making his way up the stairs to where I assumed his office was. I turned and offered my hand to Angela. "Hi Angela, good to meet you."

"You're Elaine's husband, right? We've been expecting you for a while now."

"Yeah, I got that from Gavin, but tell me, I only found out about the job today, so how is it that I was expected?"

"Oh, we told Elaine about the vacancy a couple of weeks ago and she said she'd have a chat with you about it." Angela was dressed in what I assumed to be the staff uniform. White shirt, black sweater, and black trousers. There was embroidery on the sweater which at a glance – because I didn't want to be seen to be staring at my new manager's chest – I noticed read, THE CUNRY PRODUCE STOE. I did a double take and was caught doing so by Angela. "Oh, that yeah – pointing to her left breast – the clothing supplier made a cock up with the embroidery. Some new apprentice or other, who apparently spells as she speaks. Anyway, we said we'd take them, for nothing of course, while he does us another batch."

Laughing nervously I decided to move us on. "Well lucky for me that the vacancy remained open, eh?" And with that Angela seemed to lose interest and hastily introduced me to one of my supervisors.

I turned to see a jolly young-looking lady, probably in her late twenties – also decked out in the same garb as Angela, complete with spelling error on her sweater, and seemingly keen to make my acquaintance. This was Denise, who was quick to tell me that she'd come to the shop straight from school some years ago and was only recently promoted to shop floor supervisor. Not that she'd had any previous grocery retail experience. "I was just in the right place at the right time, I guess. My mum drove me here one afternoon after school and told the manager that she wouldn't come pick me up until they'd offered me a job. She's such a kidder my mum."

This got me thinking, maybe that's why there was genuine relief on the part of Gavin following my acceptance of the job. Because the alternative was that I would become a permanent fixture in their meeting room, with Elaine refusing to come and collect me.

A most apparent thing about Denise was that as she spoke, she also chuckled at every opportunity. One of those people that uses laughter as others might use punctuation. So, as she's telling me all about her employment to the shop, where a comma, or a pause for breath would ordinarily be in a sentence, she'd let out a little chuckle.

But despite this annoying affliction, Denise was a pleasant and positive person who seemed to find joy in practically anything – all the time. In time, I was to also learn that she had the patience of a saint. Especially when it came to dealing with the badly behaved and particularly needy customers, of which there were many.

Finally, there was Fran (Francis), middle aged, white ferocious hair, probably out of a bottle, dressed in a black shirt, black trousers and a pair of black steel toe capped dealer boots which had clearly never seen a duster. Denise made the introductions and then beat a hasty retreat. Like handing a bone to a lion with toothache.

Fran was sitting near the back door on a highbacked chair – with an extra cushion on it, which over the years had taken on the shape of her not inconsiderable backside – facing a high legged table upon which stood the grubbiest computer keyboard and screen I'd ever seen in my life. I was told by Denise that she was on point, ready to receive all the goods that came into the small loading and unloading bay. One of those no-nonsense characters who, if it wasn't for the workplace no smoking rules, would have looked quite at home with a cheroot cigar hanging from the corner of her mouth. Like you might see in one of those old Clint Eastwood wild west films. Such was her presence she also wouldn't have looked out of place guarding the door of a nightclub at the dodgy end of town.

Fran gave me a brief look over. "Alright love?" then quickly turned back to berate the 'egg delivery man' for apparently being late with his deliveries, rapidly followed by, "And don't forget to take the empty egg cartons with you, we're not a storeroom you know!" Which is exactly where we were standing. In time I came to like Fran, the rottweiler with a wicked sense of humour and a heart of gold.

These introductions left just one other person that made up the management team, a supervisor by the name of Maureen. Affectionately known as Mau (pronounced 'more') or, "the real boss" as Fran was to tell me. However, she wasn't due in until the following Saturday, so our first meeting would coincide with my first day on the job.

Strange as it may sound and considering my reluctance to go along with this idea in the first place, I was starting to get a warm feeling about this new job of mine. I think it was the fact that since shaking hands with Gavin to seal our deal, and then meeting that small assortment of people in the storeroom, I hadn't stopped smiling.

Continuing to do so as Angela emerged from her small office. "Here's your apron and a spare, which you wash yourself, and you need to supply your own pens. See you Saturday morning." And once again losing interest in my company, or life in general, turned and walked away. First thing I did was to check the spelling and I'm pleased to say that all was well. As for the 'XXL one size fits no one in particular' apron, I was left wondering as to whether it was it like my school uniform of old. Where it was purposefully bought two or three sizes too big, and as the terms pass, you eventually grew into it. In my case, about six months before I left the school altogether.

As I turned towards the exit, a young lad came rushing up behind me. "Here's your coffee, sir," and proceeded to hand me a cup and saucer with equal measures of black coffee in both.

"I'm sorry, but I'm just about to leave." So, we stood facing one another… He had a cup and saucer that he needed to offload, and I really didn't want it. Making the point by keeping my hands behind my back. Finally, Fran broke the stalemate. "Pass it over here, I'll have it, and there's no need to call him sir he's no one important he's just one of us."

And that was it, in an instant I was no longer the retired IT exec I was now "one of us", and so began my next adventure.

"How'd it go?" Elaine asked as I got back into the car.

"Well, I'm sure you won't be surprised to hear that I got the job, start on Saturday as it happens. They've even given me these grocer shop styled aprons, although I have to provide my own pens apparently, a ballpoint and a permanent marker pen, so I'm told."

"There was never any doubt in my mind," she replied. With what I thought was an unnecessary look of triumph on her face.

Which got me thinking that there really wasn't any doubt that I would be working at The Country Produce Store. Even before I mentioned that I needed to come up with something to fill my time due to the ongoing planning application. Remember I told you previously that my wife is many things? Well, another one of those things is perceptive or, in this case, pre-emptive. Because she was way ahead of the game. But importantly, I had to be the one to plant the seed and that seed was the need to come up with a plan to deal with my impending unemployment. All she did was propagate it.

A talented gardener – my wife.

FOUR

MICHAEL BECOMES ACQUAINTED.

"Alright you lot, listen up, you're not being paid to stand and chat!" One of Maureen's classic opening lines in what was less of a motivational speech and more of a diatribe of demands and expectations of us for the coming ten hours. Often adding a public admonishment for anyone that hadn't met her exacting standards the previous day, or since she was last in the building.

It was Saturday morning and being keen to impress, even at my age, I arrived at seven o'clock ready for my seven-thirty shift. All scrubbed up, hair combed and my neatly pressed apron making me look like a pork loin joint: the XXL cord needed to be wound around my waist numerous times. Reassuringly tapping the pens in my top pocket, looking every bit like the imposter that I was.

All the gear, no idea.

Do you work here? – The shop floor chronicles

Having spent the previous two days going over each of the people's names with my wife, I confidently rattled off an enthusiastic (possibly too enthusiastic), "Good morning!" to the other members of the shop floor team as they arrived for work. Some whom I hadn't even met before, looked genuinely alarmed as I bounded over to them, like some over excited (large) puppy dog. As people gathered and old friends exchanged pleasantries, I had the chance to look around. The first time I was here, just after my interview, I didn't really take the place in. So, for all intents and purposes, it was my first time behind the scenes of a shop. In an instant my perspective of a shop changed from that of a customer – where, quite frankly, like most blokes, I tended to notice nothing much at all - to that of a shop floor worker, where I took in everything. And if front of house is orderly and the epitome of an environment geared up to do business, then back of house is the polar opposite. Floor to ceiling, rack upon rack of produce, stretching out as far as the eye could see. Wooden pallets, some fully loaded with just delivered stuff waiting to be attended to; some half empty, having presumably been left from the day before; boxes of produce waiting to be priced up before being put out on the shop floor; customer deliveries, customer collections; and a whole wall of walk-in fridges and freezers.

Wrenched from my reverie I was confronted by Maureen (Mau), my supervisor: the real boss. Mau had worked at the store longer than anyone else, surviving two store managers, any number of supervisors and being largely responsible (according to Fran) for the high turnover of shop floor staff. But according to Gavin, and the owners who I had the pleasure of meeting a short while later, her knowledge and the relationships she had with any number of customers was invaluable to The Country Produce Store. I'm also thinking back to my interview between Gavin's attention span and Angela's lack of interest – how much of a knowledge black hole there would be if Maureen was to leave the shop?

If ever there was a person who could charm the devil out of hell, then give him a right good telling off before sending him back down again, it was Maureen.

Physically average in many ways I guess, but if Gavin was laid back - to the point of being motionless - then Mau was his antithesis. In fact, now I think about it, the remaining management team were conspicuous by their absence as Maureen took to the floor. Moving around the store like a comet on wheels, with no time for small talk as she insisted on getting straight to the point. A no nonsense personality that exuded both confidence and firmness in equal measure. The confidence being: "I know all there is to know about this place." And firmness: "I wrote the book on all and any stunts that shop floor workers might try to pull, so don't try it on with me." I immediately liked Maureen - a lot. I sensed that behind the façade there was a person that, although authoritative, would have no qualms in standing up for her staff if the need arose. In the short term I treated Mau with both the respect and caution her personality demanded, but over time the dynamic of our relationship changed somewhat. Yes, we did cross swords on a few occasions, but I always respected the fact that she was my boss regardless of my own lofty professional background. I also acknowledged and tried (although often failed) to live up to the high standards she set herself and insisted upon from everyone else. Although in recognition of the fact that I, and everyone else for that matter, did try their best, she would often make a point of stopping you wherever you happened to be in the shop to offer a simple "Well done". High praise from Maureen, I can tell you. Which was worth its weight in carats – as in diamonds, not vegetables. It was on more than one occasion; I saw her step in if a customer was being particularly naughty (her term not mine) to any one of her shop floor team. Though if whatever she had been forced to bail you out of on the shop floor was in any way your fault, and could have been avoided, you'd know about it. Maureen did nothing that wasn't in the best interests of The Country Produce Store, her subordinates and/or the customers. Pretty much in that order.

Seemingly without a need to exchange pleasantries, she quickly introduced herself. "You must be Michael, well I'm Maureen. You've probably already heard the rumours about me, most of which I'm in no doubt are true. Either way I don't care. I'm employed to do a job and so are you. And as long as we both remember that, and who's in charge, we'll get along really fine. You'll be shadowing Ross today, learn as much as you can. But if you have any questions then you know where I am."

"Do I?"

"Yes Michael, right behind you!"

Ross, a particularly tall, Canadian bloke was soon to leave The Country Produce Store, so, according to Mau, I needed to learn all I could from him between now and then. As if on cue Ross stepped forward. "Morning Mau, morning Michael, good to meet you…," but was cut off in midsentence by the whirlwind, "No time for that Ross, just make sure you teach Michael all you know. You've got three days, which should be plenty of time." Going on to tell us. "Oh, and don't forget your radio. Don't let me catch any of you" – pausing and moving her steely gaze around the room – "on the shop floor without your radio, we need to be able to contact you at all times. Any questions? – No? Good. Off you go then." I fully expected her to go on and tell us, "Stay safe out there," as they often do on the American cop shows, but she didn't.

As we were leaving the stockroom Ross was to tell me that the particular piece of advice regarding the radios was given at the beginning of every shift, regardless of how long you had worked there. "So just nod, agree and make sure you take a radio. In fact, I suggest where Mau is concerned you just nod and agree with everything she says."

As the door to the stockroom closed behind us, I could still hear Maureen turning her attention to the rest of the shop floor team. Quickly reeling off a whole list of misdemeanours, things to do and things she needed attending to. Those assigned to the checkouts (tills) would need to know and read up on any new products, plus a whole plethora of watchouts and new rules. I was also introduced to a whole new glossary of terms, such as; backstock, deadstock, private labelling, visual merchandising and so many others that I had no clue of on that first day.

And that was it, everyone was dismissed. Or rather Maureen simply turned around and proceeded to get on with whatever she needed to do next.

Ross and I continued on up the shop floor. "That was some pep talk," I said.

"Don't worry about Mau, her bark's worse than her bite. Not that she's ever bitten anyone mind, although she's come close a few times I reckon." All said in a confident Canadian accent and with a huge grin on his huge face. During my time on this Earth of ours I reckon I've come across quite a variety of head shapes and sizes, most of which I've never really given a second thought to. But Ross's was unique. Imagine if you can a large, boiled ham – constantly grinning. That was Ross.

Being on the shop floor for the first time as an employee, as opposed to a shopper is an odd experience. All of a sudden, I'm now part of this retail machine. Not necessarily a modern machine mind you, but one that has been designed with endurance in mind. Like one of those old steam engines that you might see at the local country fair, or a steam railway train perhaps: a bit clunky, old fashioned, quaint even, but nonetheless reliable and, in its own way, beautiful. Year on year people will turn out and marvel at it, long after its successors have themselves been superseded many times over.

Which brings to mind another of Mau's morning motivational speeches. On this particular occasion she was to impress upon us her views relating to the modern world of retail which had no place at The Country Produce Store. "Fashionable bandwagons and other such miraculous breakthroughs are not as progressive as you might think. You'll know what I mean if you've had the misfortune to have worked in a supermarket. Look what's happened to them…"

Becky, one of the more outspoken members of our team and therefore likely to have a very limited 'stay employed' date, responded. "I think you'll find that many supermarkets are quite innovative Maureen."

"Exactly! And where is that getting them eh? Let me tell you. Nowhere that is good for our proud traditions." Then, not allowing further discussion to ensue, she instantly vacated the space occupied just a second before.

But the shop floor, underneath its old and new vaulted roof, is almost cathedral like. The perimeter, until it meets either the delicatessen, the butchery counter or the considerable bank of fridges and freezers is a shelved wooden wonderland, offering literally hundreds of different types and makes of foodstuffs. Some branded goods, that are well-known to the regular shopper, some not so well known, and many unique to this type of environment. Particularly those that claim to be derived from an artisan of sorts. But there is one common thread that runs through most of the produce on offer and that is the exorbitant price. "But it's not about the price Michael," Sharon, a no-nonsense Irish colleague once told me. "As I was told when I first started here – people don't come here just to buy food they come here for an experience."

"What the experience of getting your pocket picked as you gaze aloft at the nineteenth century oak beams you mean?"

"Now you're getting it." All said with that classic touch of Irish irony.

Hanging by wires throughout the store are an assortment of 'swing signs' many of which are delightfully and uniquely agricultural. Above the butchery there were numerous signs, with two in particular showing similar pictures of four or five piglets with their little pink heads resting on top of a hay bale. The first had a caption which read 'Made to order pork skewers for your BBQ' and the other 'Pork pies from our Happy Pigs farm'.

Others around the shop included the ever-popular picture of a field full of cattle with the sun dipping (or rising) on the horizon, telling us that 'meat is neat for your health', apparently; 'British is Best' cunningly hung above the French, and German cheese display; and a picture showing a young farming couple and who I took to be their two children, one each side of mum and dad. All four family members standing in a field somewhere in Britain and the caption reading 'Pasture fed, hand reared and properly aged'. There wasn't an animal in sight. I'm thinking (or hoping) that this must have been one of a set of pictures where no doubt animals would have featured, but on its own...? My favourite though, was the one pinned to the wall behind the butchery counter which Pete, the head butcher, was keen to explain to me. "So, during a meeting Gavin announced that he felt that we needed to be hipper and cooler. He asked us what we thought about changing how our staff are referred to. We thought he was joking, until that is he came up with the new label. I even made a joke about it to try and make him see how it might be construed, but he just didn't get it. Then a few hours later he's handing me this sign, insisting I pin it up straightway. 'For Allergen Advice – Please feel free to reach out to your nearest member'. "The lads, particularly young Gary, would often be heard asking if anyone would like some allergen advice."

And finally 'Any form of abuse to staff will not be tolerated' – later changed to read 'Any form of abuse to our members will not be tolerated' which many of our customers took as a challenge.

Every available inch of floor space across the shop is taken up with displays on tables and standalone shelf units of what I discovered to be speciality and seasonal goods. Less artisan and more trappings for the tourist. If you want a cuddly bear for the price of a meal for two, with the name The Country Produce Store embroidered across its chest, then look no further than one of these display units. Alternatively, if you're looking for a locally sourced, made in China, teapot then step right up.

But this was my first day and I'm now on the footplate of this grand old machine along with the rest of my shop floor colleagues. All in our designated positions waiting for the day's journey to begin. All that is missing is the steam whistle. Instead, we have a 'Mau horn'. "Come on you lot, no time for chit chat let's get the shop open!" And off she flies to inspect the table displays and shelf units, as if wearing roller blades and a rocket pack.

* * *

Following in Ross's considerable shadow, I was told that the first jobs of the day included uncovering the fruit and veg and wheeling the trolleys outside to take up residence along the store front for the day. All needing to be done before I was properly introduced to a whole bunch of other people who weren't in our immediate shop floor team, such as the butchery and coffee shop people.

As we were heading towards the door with a snake of about six trolleys each, Ross enquires of me. "So what shop did you work in before you came here then Mike? In other words, what can I skip in terms of what I need to show you versus what you probably know already?"

"That's easy." I reply, "you don't have to skip anything, because I know bugger all."

"You serious?!"

"Yep, never worked in a shop before."

"You do realise that I'm leaving on Tuesday and that you're meant to be me from there on in, right?"

"I do now. I mean, I knew you were leaving but that's about it. Oddly enough it never came up at my interview that I was to be the new you. Just as a matter of interest, you're not moving anywhere near to Dunstone Town are you?"

"No, why? Where is that?"

"I've no idea, it came up in my interview that's all."

We carried on wheeling the trolleys outside and then came back in to uncover the fruit and veg, stowing the covers in a cleverly concealed cupboard under one of the shelf units.

I felt like I really needed to gain this man's confidence, somehow let him know that I wasn't a complete retail moron. Therefore, as we were neatly folding the polythene covers, I ventured. "So Ross, I'm guessing that the trolleys will need to be wheeled back in later and the fruit and veg covered up before we head home tonight, right?" I've heard people say there's no such thing as a stupid question, and here I was proving that theory wrong, but I needed to start somewhere and, in doing so, keep within the limits of my current knowledge of anything retail.

With unconcealed cynicism. "Man you're a natural, I can see there'll be no pulling the wool over your eyes Mike. You figure that all out for yourself? Good job!"

With sarcasm being laid on so thickly even I was able to detect it. I shouldn't have been surprised, though at least I knew where we stood now, which is always a good thing in any new job. Which had me wondering whether now would be a good time to mention the boiled ham thing. I looked at him, gave him my best 'yeah whatever' smile, took in his lumberjack sized frame and decided to keep my thoughts to myself and my mouth shut – for now.

The fruit and vegetables were of the utmost importance. According to Ross they were one of the principal showcases of the store, along with the butchery and delicatessen. Therefore, the display and produce had to not only look good but needed to be policed throughout the day to ensure that they stayed that way. They also needed to be constantly replenished. But we were to come back to that a little later as Ross decided to make a detour and do some more introductions. First port of call was the coffee shop.

"So, Alison this is Michael, he's taking over from me."

"Hi, so are you a Michael or a Mike?" says Alison.

Stepping out of the shadow I replied, "Either is fine and great to meet you."

With that, a door opens from what I see is a kitchenette, and out walks another lady with her red hair tied back in the severest of ponytails. So tight I'm thinking that if that ponytail was to ever come loose her face would probably fold in on itself.

"Morning Ali," says Ross, "this is Michael, he started this morning and is to be my replacement. Michael, meet our other Alison."

"Hi, so are you a Michael or a Mike?" says Other Alison.

"Either, not fussed really and great to meet you too. So, tell me Alison – and Alison, do I call you both the same name or …?"

"Oh, I see where you're going with this," says Ross. "first off we don't do formal round here, so we call both our Alison's Ali."

"I'm not sure that's helping."

To which he says, as if it was obvious all along. "So this is Ginger Ali, and this is Skinny Ali".

Are they serious? I'm sure there's a Harry Potter joke in there somewhere but I can't quite figure out the punchline yet...

"Of course, they are!" With little else left to say, as I consider how this comedy sketch might play out, I simply grin. As I'm grinning inanely Gavin appears. "Good morning, all. I hear that runner beans might be in short supply this coming Christmas, what do you think?"

Ross is the first to react. "But it's only February Gavin, how could anyone possibly know that? Or is this just another one of those random comments of yours?"

"Random comments? I have no idea to what you're referring." Then turning his head toward me. "Mike, is that a grin on your face or trapped wind? Because you know what I say about people's smiles don't you?"

"Yes that was a grin Gavin, leftover from a previous conversation, and sorry no I have no idea what you say about people's smiles." Looking at the others for some hint as to what he was going on out, but they looked equally as bemused, with ny Ali confirming as much with a shrug of her y shoulders.

"Your smile reflects the positive reputation of our shop, an extension to our motto if you like." Said as though he were preaching from a pulpit.

Recalling my interview. "What the moto on the wall in the meeting room, 'welcome to the funny farm'?"

I was left to assume that the effort of walking the shop floor and engaging in conversation left Gavin needing a recharge, because rather than comment further, he instead walked on towards the stockroom. I turned to each of my new colleagues looking for some clue as to what had just happened. Ross was the first to speak. "Well Mike, congratulations! Just twenty minutes into your first day on the job and you've been Gavined. I think that's a record." As he spoke, he received a nodding confirmation from both the Ali's that I'd inadvertently broken some record or other.

I was then introduced to the Saturday help, a tall thin lad called Ben. I recall that this was the same lad who tried to insist that I take a cup and saucer full of coffee from him as I was about to leave the building, following my interview. It turned out that he was a student at the local tech college, apparently studying theatre prop making. I was inclined to ask more about this endeavour of his, but he was clearly uncomfortable with the whole business of meeting people, so I simply offered my hand in the normal way that gentlemen usually do when they meet –

albeit for the second time. For a few seconds I was left hanging, until – with none of the youthful vigour I would have expected from such a young man – he offered his hand up, whilst keeping his eyes firmly fixed onto my shoes. "Hi Ben, good to meet you - again," I explained to the others how we had met previously, "how are you today?" Clearly needing time to consider his answer he moved his gaze to my face, said nothing, smiled and walked back behind the safety of the coffee shop counter. I was left wondering whether the Ali's kept a little wicker basket under the counter for him to sleep in, as you might a puppy dog.

Ross broke the ensuing silence. "We'll do the butchers later, because we need to get on with the fruit and veg before the shop starts to get too busy."

* * *

The rules surrounding the provision and care of the fruit and vegetables were numerous and I found myself needing to take notes. In summary, each morning, and periodically throughout the day, it all gets checked for quality. Anything not passing muster is removed, reduced, or wasted off. With the latter either offered to the staff and/or then disposed of. After which, the wooden display boxes are replenished with whatever fresh fruit and vegetables there happens to be in stock. Deliveries normally came in three times a week, sometimes four depending on sales. Although there were some additional deliveries, but these were usually only at Easter and Christmas.

So how is 'passing muster' measured, what are

the guidelines and so on? Well, here's a brief extract from Ross's 'The guide to inspecting fruit and vegetables for dummies.' You won't find it in any bookshop or online, because it's all in the man's extraordinarily large head. "Right Mike, first things first, if you look at a piece of fruit or a vegetable and think to yourself, 'I'd never buy that' then remove it. Now, some of what you pull out might be worth just reducing in price and putting back out, but making sure you put it to one side, never mix reduced stuff with the fresh stuff. For example, take these courgettes. When they start to look and feel as soft as an old man's penis then it's probably time to pull them off. Same for these satsumas, when they're looking like an old scrotum, then … What are you laughing at?"

"Sorry, nothing, got it, old man's penis, pull them off and remove scrotum, understood. Carry on please." Frantically scribbling nothing legible in my little notebook. This was definitely going to be one of those indelible memories. A moment in time that was up there with, my children being born, passing my driving test, getting married (both times) and having sex for the first time. But not necessarily in that order.

And so, we went through the whole range of fruit and vegetables with Ross giving me the benefit of his years of experience in the art of appraising the health of each type and grading most according to an aging piece of either human anatomy, or that of a farmyard animal; with me standing just out of shot with a stupid boyish grin on my face. Subsequently I was to discover that many fruits and vegetables, those that are considered as being beneficial for certain parts of our body, do actually resemble that particular body part. Check it out. That said, I'm not suggesting for one minute that Ross applied any kind of science to his appraisal process. So probably best to leave it at that before any elderly gentlemen reading this sees some tenuous connection between vegetables and getting pulled off.

Later in the morning came my introduction to the butchery lads. As we walked past the counter the head butcher, Pete, called out to Ross – and all and any customers in the shop at the time. "New boy then Ross, looks a bit older than you're used to. If you need a hand breaking him in, then give us a shout." All said as he was hammering the hell out of a piece of cod fat.

In case you're wondering: *Cod fat is taken from the scrotum / crotch area of beef cattle and reputed to be behind the naming of the cod piece. The same cod piece that was popular in Europe in the 15th and 16th centuries. The pouchlike addition to men's long hose (look that up if you don't know), located at the crotch.*

Smiling politely, I gave Pete a manly thumbs up and offered back, "Good to meet you too Pete, you look like a man who clearly knows how to beat his meat."

With a huge grin on his face, and not missing a beat, he shouted back, "Twice a week mate, twice a week. With or without the missus." Laughing raucously.

At least I learnt how low the bawdy bar was set in

the shop.

* * *

On the small delicatessen there was my wife Elaine, the architect of my current situation, and her sidekick Helen. A jolly person, corn fed and oven ready inside her snug fitting regulation XXL apron. Both seemed to rub along together, and ever keen to share their extensive knowledge of cheese, pâté, and pies to any passer-by, whether they have a particular interest or not. My wife's passion for cheese and all things delicatessen is legendary in our house. Even more so than her passion for my continued employment. Our one-sided debates on the merits of French cheese, which is overrated by all accounts, and English cheese, which is underrated, have sometimes stretched well into the evening and even to bedtime. And whatever you do, don't get her started on Scotch eggs. It's not so much the thing itself that cheeses her off (see what I did there?) it's when people come along and ask for a "Scots egg", or "Scottish egg" or some other variation.

This being one of her favourite tales. "We're going to visit friends in Scotland, so as a joke we thought we'd take them some Scots eggs made here in England. We thought about buying a kilt, but we couldn't find one anywhere around here." Said a lady of some years with thinning blue rinsed hair, and a face and voice that has lived through the smoke of a thousand (or more) high tar cigarettes.

Being ever the politest of people, my wife, she rarely says to people what she is actually thinking. Such as there being no such thing as a Scots egg. Not unless you're referring to an actual egg that belongs to a person of Scotland. So I wasn't surprised to hear that on this particular occasion, she chose a more quiescent delivery. "If you mean Scotch eggs then you're in luck because we have quite a few on sale today. How many would you like, madam?" Adding, for good measure, and improving her customer's knowledge (although not necessarily her manner), "you might be interested to know that Scotch eggs are probably not Scottish in origin."

"So why are they called Scots then?" One of many things to know about customers, of a particular type, is that they rarely listen. Much the same as when a bloke asks for directions to somewhere or other, and then instantly forgets a few seconds after they've been told. Or is that just me?

"Since you ask, I remember reading somewhere that Scotch eggs were apparently invented a long time ago in England." I told you; she knows her stuff my wife.

But not having the energy or inclination to go on to say that: *it doesn't seem to be entirely clear as to exactly where Scotch eggs originated. Wikipedia tell us it was in the North of England – Whitby Yorkshire to be precise. Other commentators say it was at Fortnum & Mason in London sometime during the 18th century. The Encyclopaedia Britannica goes as far as to suggest that its origin was northern India. However, the one thing they all agree on is that the Scotch egg is NOT a Scottish invention.*

"Oh! Well now you've put the kibosh on that little joke, perhaps you have something else that we can take instead?"

Polite, to the point of becoming aggravated, Elaine suggested the following: "Certainly madam. We do have some haggis in the cold cabinet that I believe may have been invented *and* made in Scotland, though imported to England a few weeks ago. Perhaps you could take some of that back with you when you go?" Thinking but not saying, 'It doesn't really sell too well to be honest, so you'd be doing us a favour.' As far as the delicatessen is concerned, both Helen and Elaine find themselves having to navigate around as many annoying situations as there are challenging ones. Similar to the shop floor, I guess. Although often unique in nature, due largely to the huge selection of products they offer in such a relatively small space. The most common annoyance being the self-appointed experts and pompous arses that enjoy nothing more than sharing their very limited knowledge of some cheese or other with a pair of actual experts – Elaine and Helen.

Apart from the Scotch Egg Brigade there's another thing that for some reason really gets under Elaine's skin: the mispronunciation of 'Quiche'. I know, but that's my wife for you. The most common mispronunciations coming out as either "quish" or "kish". As annoying as *she* finds it, I actually find it quite amusing to hear, especially the pompous sorts, asking for a slice of kish with that (false) air of knowing what they're talking about when it comes to fine dining. Not that Quiche of any type would necessarily be considered as fine dining in my book. But each to their own, I guess.

As I say, there are many annoyances…

"Your chicken and mushroom pies."

"Yes, madam, they are particularly popular today. All the ingredients are locally sourced and the pies themselves are baked fresh every day in the small artisan bakery next door."

"I really enjoyed the filling, but I'm not so keen on the pastry, can I have a pie without the pastry please?"

"But then it wouldn't be a pie madam, it would just be some pie filling."

"Yes, I know, that's what I'm asking, can you sell me some pie filling?"

"No madam, we can't do that. Anything else I can help you with today?"

Here's another one of the many things to know about customers, and that is when they don't get their own way it is generally perceived to be down to the failings of the shop and its staff (or members). Because not only have they got it in to their heads that they are always right, but they are also blameless. And my dog is a juggler. But unlike Gavin he does have balls.

* * *

Briefly back to cheese, and taking you forward a few months…

I was having a proper bad day when Pete the butchery manager suggested that they could name a cheese after me. On one of the few days when the antics of a selection of our customers really got to me

Do you work here? – The shop floor chronicles

Pete was on the deli with Helen in deep conversation about some smoked sausage or other (nothing implied). Head down, shoulders hunched, trying to avoid any form of human contact, I endeavoured to pass by the deli undetected. But there was no getting away from Pete. "Now there's a face that could curdle milk. In fact, I'd go as far as to say you could use that face to make cheese."

Across the country cheese seems to have adopted all manner of quirky names. Or perhaps they've always had them and it's only because of my recent appointment that I now have an increased awareness of such things. You may have heard of many of these oddly named cheeses yourself such as: Stinking Bishop, Drunken Hooligan, Ticklemore, Slack Ma Girdle and a whole range of others.

Within the same spirit and looking at my 'milk curdling' face, Pete came up with, in his usual town crier manner. "How about 'Miserable Fucker'?" And with Helen – now an accomplice – and firmly on board with the idea. "I'm thinking it would be a heavy blue cheese, I reckon, what do you think?" – A probable reference to my waistline and mood. "Yeah, you're right, but with an unpleasant texture." – A realistic reference to my customer facing skills. "And likely to leave a bad taste in your mouth," – Not sure what that was a reference to. Oh, and according to both of them, 'Miserable Fucker' should definitely not be made available for public consumption.

Truth is, I was to quickly learn, old scrotums aside for the moment, that most of the shop floor people possessed a much-needed sense of humour, as well as both passion and a huge amount of knowledge of many of the products sold throughout the shop. And, if I was to be an accepted and valuable member of this team, I needed to up my game and develop a thick skin - fast!

* * *

The staff restroom was some distance from the shop floor which was good. Not so good was that it was adjacent to Gavin's office and the only staff toilet in the building. And neither were particularly welcoming. Grubby, unsanitary and with an aroma of aged farts emanating from it. And the toilet wasn't much better either. The staff restroom, an oxymoron, was cleverly designed to provide its users with zero comfort. Half a dozen or so hard plastic chairs, that caused your backside to sweat after just a few minutes, surrounded a Formica topped table which, from looking at the edges, I could see once sported a pretty floral pattern. At one end of the table there was a collection of old Sunday supplement magazines. One of which carried the headline – Say no to decimal currency! A staff noticeboard on a wall, with a banner across the top that read: Company notices only. And underneath an array of memos and A4 posters ranging from; Don't forget your Christmas raffle tickets to details of the forthcoming Halloween party – It was February. There was also a Ford Fiesta for sale, albeit a couple of years ago.

Occupying one corner was a kitchenette. No cooker but the mandatory microwave with the interior showing all the signs of a thousand exploding ready meals and homemade soups. A sink containing the detritus of this morning's tea and coffee run and a cupboard underneath housing all manner of cleaning fluids, clothes, and spare toilet rolls.

As the newbie, I would be expected to do the washing up at the end of the day, having already been put on point this morning to make the tea and coffee for all of my shop floor colleagues and the management team. Within a wall cupboard above the sink, I found the mug collection. Personal ones brought in from home and many others likely given away as freebies by sales reps. Most cracked and chipped, and all stained brown. As far as the success of my first tea run was concerned, it was a bit of a mixed bag if I'm being honest. Having had the forethought to write down the various requirements, tea, coffee, black, white, sugar, not sugar, sweetener, milk substitute and so on, I genuinely thought I was on to a winner. However, what I didn't legislate for, and allegedly considered as gross misconduct, was giving people their beverage in the wrong mug. There are a significant number of synonyms for incompetent and idiot. And by ten thirty that morning I was all of them.

My first lunchtime, and as a kind of celebration of the event I decided to treat myself to a meat pasty from the deli. But, as much I was looking forward to it, and even with my staff discount, I couldn't get over the fact that at my current payrate it would take me the best part of an hour to recover the cost. Sitting across the table from Ross gave me an opportunity to have a non-shop conversation. "So, was there a life before The Country Produce Store, Ross?"

"Do you want the true answer, or my stock answer?"

"There's a difference?"

"Yep and, as I'm leaving, I'll let you in on both. The true answer is that I used to be an electrician, but my knees gave out, so I had to give it up. Thing is if I let on that I'm an electrician then people start to ask me all sorts of DIY questions, wanting advice or wanting me to do work for them. Even after I've explained about my knees."

"So, what do you do?"

"Well, that's where my stock answer comes into play. I tell people that I'm a retired gynaecologist. So, no more DIY questions, no requests for advice and most certainly no one wanting me to come to their homes and do work for them. How's your pasty?"

"Hi, you guys, taking a well-earned rest I see. Looks like brown shoes are coming back into fashion. What do you reckon?" And with that Gavin breezes past and into his office leaving me to stare at his back and Ross shrugging as if nothing of note had happened.

"So how about you Mike, what's your story?"

Having not yet prepared an alternative stock answer I revealed that I'd spent thirty plus years in IT, then retired. Or at least that was the plan. As if fired out of a cannon Gavin appeared from his office. "IT you say. Well, let me tell you that we have nothing but problems with our IT here. Only yesterday my PC went down on me four times."

Do you work here? – The shop floor chronicles

For the avoidance of any doubt. PC in the context of this anecdote is Personal Computer and not Peace Corps or Police Constable. Or at least I assumed so.

Ross was on it in a flash, "l'homme et la machine en parfaite harmonie."

I then spent the remaining fifteen minutes of my first lunchbreak listening to all manner of agonies (or ecstasies) allegedly caused by computers. And all the while watching the grinning boiled ham across the table out the corner of my eye.

"Gavin, maybe we can pick this up another time as sadly my lunchtime has finished already. And look, I haven't even had the time to finish my artisan meat pasty." With that Pete emerged from the toilet and, doing the maths, I estimated that he'd been in there for a minimum of my thirty-minute lunchbreak. How long before we sat down for lunch I wasn't to know. What he'd been doing in all that time was a superfluous question, as all was revealed at the point at which he emerged from the single door separating the restroom from the toilet.

A hasty exit and down to the shop floor with a third of my lunch in my pocket Maureen appeared and made an emergency stop in front of me. "No food to be taken onto the shop floor Michael."

* * *

The rest of my first day came and went and, before I knew where I was it was time to close the shop. Which is when I was to make – First Contact.

Having made the astute observation earlier in the day that the trolleys would need to be wheeled back inside the shop later, I was permitted to carry out this most uncomplicated of tasks unsupervised.

"Hey, you there! Do you work here?" The bark belonged to an elderly lady alighting from the passenger door of a large, British, executive 4x4 – I'm sure you know the one I'm referring to. Which incidentally had missed the carpark by a considerable distance, having chosen instead to park with its nose almost touching the shop entrance. She was splendidly dressed in a full-length waxed coat and a pair of ™Hunter wellingtons that had clearly never seen the great outdoors.

Looking down at my grocer's apron and specifically at the large blue letters on the left of my chest which read 'THE COUNTRY PRODUCE STORE', I felt pretty confident, as I pointed at the said letters. "Yes madam, I do work here." And in doing so giving her one of my warmest smiles. The type of smile that said, "although I've been here for less than a day, I'm feeling pretty good about myself right now".

"Are you just closing?" She asked.

"No madam we always bring the trolleys in at certain times of the day to make it harder for customers to shop." Now that would have been a great response, but what I actually said was. "No madam we aren't just closing we are in fact closed."

"But I need to buy a few things for our supper."

"Unfortunately, the tills are all closed and everyone's going home, because it's our closing time."

Do you work here? – The shop floor chronicles

"But I need to buy a few things for our supper."
The woman repeated, perhaps thinking that I hadn't
heard first time round.

Or did I, at some point, inadvertently break into
an obscure language? Why I would do such a thing
I'm not quite sure, mainly because I don't know any
obscure languages. But then it *was* late in the day. I
decided to try again, being sure to speak in English
this time. In doing so I delivered the same message
but with fewer words. "Yes, I understand that
madam, but we are in fact closed now."

Yep, definitely English that time and all said
without letting the obligatory smile slip from my
face. Remembering the gist of what Gavin was
telling us about earlier – smile, reputation, motto,
funny farm. However, despite my best efforts, she
persisted. "But I need to buy a few things for our
supper."

I was at a bit of a loss if I'm being honest, and I
looked around the shop for some assistance, but there
was no one to be seen. Maybe I was missing
something? Perhaps it was her that was struggling
with the English language. I mean I was told that we
do get foreign visitors coming in from time to time.
So, was this a case in point? If so, then it could be
that what she keeps saying to me are the only words
she knows.

With that, Ross appeared. "Everything okay
Mike?"

"Yep, all good, just trying to help this lady out –
literally. In fact, now you're here, and what with it
being my first day and all, perhaps you could help me

out?" Without waiting for an answer, I turned to the lady and said, very slowly (just in case). "This-is-my-supervisor-madam, I'm-sure-that-he-can-help-you-with-your-enquiry." With that, and ignoring Ross's strange look, I bid her a lovely evening and then hightailed it round the corner to give the apple and ginger chutney my most special attention.

In the background I could hear - "yes I understand madam, but we're closed …"

"But I need to buy a few things for our supper."

As it turns out she wasn't foreign after all. But one of those entitled sorts that I was soon to get a lot more experience with, and which I'll tell you more about later.

* * *

I remember the end of my first day as if it were yesterday. The same way in which some people recall, even many years later, their first proper job or day at school. Apparently, it's all down to something called 'Episodic memory'. According to those in the know it is the ability to recall and mentally reexperience specific episodes from your past. As opposed to something called 'Semantic memory' which refers to the capacity for recollecting general knowledge. Just the type of person you need in your pub quiz team. I have no idea why I've just shared that with you. Sure it will come back to me later.

Anyway, there was Elaine waiting for me at The Country Produce Store equivalent of the school gates. Sitting in the car at the rear of the shop waiting for her little soldier to come running out, clutching the first of many unfathomable masterpieces to stick on the fridge door. Only it wasn't quite like that. In fact, it was nothing remotely like that. "How was your first day? You okay? You look like you're in pain."

"The day was interesting, humorous at times, but my back and feet really ache." In fact, I had more than an ache or theatrical hobble, it was seriously debilitating. Now I know that blokes have a tendency, according to women that is, to overstate any type of pain. Often going on to play the "you should try having children" card, attempting to humiliate us out of our sickbed. But, on this occasion, giving birth would have been a welcome alternative to the pain in my lower back. But, to give Elaine her due, she didn't mention childbirth at all as I fell into the car. "Yeah working on the shop floor for ten hours will do that. I get backache most days but clearly not as bad as you. As for the sore feet that'll go away in time so long as you have the correct footwear, which you do, because I chose them for you."

As we were driving home, I was quite happy to stew in my own sympathy but being a captive audience, I was subject to all manner of advice. "Maybe you ought to buy one of those lumbar braces," continuing with, "perhaps do some special exercises, in order to build up your core strength," and the old classic, "maybe lose a few pounds."

I had never heard my wife mention her backache before. "So how is it your backache isn't as bad as mine?" Regretting asking the question as soon as it fell out of my mouth. "Who's to say it isn't?"

Thinking some more on her unrequested advice there was just one tiny thing on the list I needed to explore. "When you said, maybe lose a few pounds, were you suggesting I'm fat?"

And the car fell silent.

Over time my feet did stop aching and yes, I did buy a lumbar brace. I even tried a few of the core strengthening exercises that I found online. But the backache persisted, and I learnt not to mention it again. Although that didn't stop Elaine occasionally dropping it into the conversation on our rides home, almost goading me. "How's the back today then?"

"Holding up thanks, shall we put the radio on?"

But I learnt that many of my colleagues suffered from the dreaded backache. Only difference being – they kept it to themselves. As indeed I learnt to do.

FIVE

GETTING TO GRIPS WITH THE OTHER KIDS IN THE PLAYGROUND

Unfortunately, the 'First Contact' I described to you in the previous chapter wasn't the one-off that I had hoped it would be. During my time at The Country Produce Store, I was to have a few unhealthy run-ins with many of what I'd come to term as 'The Entitled' or 'The Belligerents'. I recently read that the term 'Entitled' is being given to the Millennials and Generation-Z types. A view, I hasten to add, often handed to them by those that *I* am choosing to call 'The Entitled'. Predominantly – although not necessarily – elderly people (Baby Boomers, or thereabouts) who are typically quite well-off and seemingly have no need to be civil, particularly to those of us in service. They also seemed to have a natural aptitude for belligerence. As if shop floor workers were nobody of consequence, invisible even.

Maybe believing we should face the wall, as servants were often expected to do back in the glorious 'olden' days. Until such times as your assistance is required. At which point, when questioned, your answer must always be exactly what it is they want to hear. The other thing I can tell you about 'The Entitled' is that wealth and age does not necessarily equal common-sense, intellect or decent manners. Following any guidelines such as: *'Please do not touch'*, *'This way to the till'*, *'Please return trolleys to where you found them'*, are typically not understood or purposely ignored. They're also particularly good at disregarding directional arrows. I refer specifically to those intended to guide people safely around the carpark. Or in the case of the COVID pandemic, when people were encouraged to follow a designated route around the shop, for safe distancing purposes.

Although my favourite of all was the sign at The Country Produce Store checkout *'Please wait to be called forward'*. Because quite a few of them just didn't get it. Although to be fair to 'The Entitled' they weren't the only ones. Many, I suspect, just chose not to get it. I was to witness other customers in the queue politely bringing the signage to the miscreant's attention, all to no avail as they continue to march up to the till regardless. Quite often standing on the shoulder – figuratively speaking of course – of the customer being served. I recall one such lady, possibly (hopefully) picking up on the look I was giving her as I was serving someone else. "Sorry am I pushing in?" As though she didn't know exactly what she was doing. "No not yet madam, but almost." Always remembering to maintain a smile which served to baffle them no end.

I witnessed similar behaviour during a trip to my local supermarket at the height of the COVID pandemic. You may recall how shops had put in place several precautions to protect both customers and its own shop floor people. Things such as sanitising stations allowing people to clean the handles on the trolley before use, sensible or social distancing measures and so on. Another such precaution was where people were encouraged to load their shopping on to the conveyers one at a time, with the next customer being expected to hang back the recommended two metres until the former had cleared the checkout entirely. The problem of course was those people I term as *'The Spanners'*.

Spanners – *As in spanner in the works. Someone that prevents something happening in the way that it was planned or prescribed. And in doing so cause a problem or difficulty for others. Or in this context – A stupid person with a tendency to act disrespectfully.*

And The Spanners, in this particular case, are the people that decide for themselves that such rules and precautions are unnecessary and most definitely not intended for them.

There is a point to all this, I promise, and here it comes.

Who was it that was left to continually enforce the rules, and in doing so take all the verbal flack that came with it? Here's a clue: It most certainly wasn't the instruction givers – probably to be found in an office somewhere – and nor was it those in government that set the rules in the first place. It would of course have been the shop floor worker at the checkout. Who, even with the plastic screen that they were sitting behind, were still risking their own wellbeing by turning out to provide the spanners, and the rest of us, with that most essential of basic services during a global health crisis.

Don't get me wrong I don't have a chip on my shoulder when it comes to wealthy or aged people. I'm on the edge of being a baby boomer myself as it happens and many of our friends are quite wealthy. But I have no time, regardless of rank, wealth, or status for rude people (and spanners).

I think I have set the tone for the rest of the book now.

SIX

MICHAEL DISCOVERS THAT IT'S NEVER TOO LATE TO
LEARN OR TO BE RIDICULOUS IT WOULD SEEM.

"Michael are you busy?"

One of the most provocative questions in the
English language I reckon, and full of trip hazards.
Especially when the interrogator is Maureen. The
problem I have with it is that there is no desirable
response. If I was to answer, "No not particularly."
Then a barrage will likely open up as to why not. On
the other hand, if I say, "Yes I am," then I would need
to prepare myself for an interrogation as to exactly
what it is I (think) am doing. Knowing all the while
that whatever it is it won't be the thing she had in
mind for me.

As much as my first day was memorable,
primarily because it was my first day, subsequent
days and weeks became a blur of events, routines,
interspersed with a touch of tedium. Over the course

of the next few weeks I was to learn an awful lot more about the world of retail. Or at least the world of retail according to The Country Produce Store. I was also becoming more confident, although never diffident by nature. What I mean is, I was a lot more self-confident around the shop.

As far as daily routines were concerned, I was well and truly getting into the groove and I also knew where things were. Largely due, in no small part, to having to do one of the most monotonous tasks in the world of retail. I refer to stock replenishment, or replen (if you were an old hand), or backstock or shelf stacking – depending on who asked us to do it. On this occasion it was Maureen.

Having stumbled over the question of how busy I was or wasn't. "From the sounds of things Michael you don't seem too clear as to whether you're busy or not. So let me help you out. Have you done replen yet?"

"Yeah, I did a bit with Ross just before he left, but I'm no expert." Hoping that by admitting to being an incompetent she'd move on. But not a chance.

"In which case I strongly suggest that you need more practice, and you know what they say about practice Michael?"

"Practice makes perfect?"

"Yes, I've heard that one too, but I was thinking more along the lines of practice makes for continued employment."

"Ah that old classic."

And so, Maureen proceeded to tell me exactly

how the replen system works and in doing so telling me to forget everything that Ross had told me because she was pretty sure that it wouldn't have been correct.

"Michael I strongly suggest that you immerse yourself in the stock replenishment programme [like I had a choice]. So, listen up because I dislike repeating myself." For the next ten minutes or so I was (literally) her captive audience. "Each part of the shop is categorised and replenished according to the type of goods. For example, one category is condiments, others are marmalades, pickles, chutneys and so on. You start at rack A – pointing at the nearest rack of produce in the stockroom – and we systematically replenish the whole shop moving down the racks going from A to B then C and so on. This should, depending on how busy we are, take anything from three to four days to complete. Not that you'll be expected to do the whole shop, others will also take a turn. Once all points have been replenished we then go all the way back to the beginning – point A and start the process all over again. Got that? Good off you go then. Oh, by the way, I know it's commonsense but the soonest sell by dates go towards the front of the shelf. Got it? Yes? Good, see you later then.

Without further ado, checking I had my radio with me, I set off towards rack A. But she wasn't quite finished with me yet, "Oh, and Michael, remember I have eyes everywhere, so no cutting corners okay!"

"Got it yes, see you later." Quickly moving away from her icy gaze to go warm up before I set about taking on my first solo run at replen.

It turns out that the stock replenishment programme was less of a system and more of a never-ending cycle of restocking the shelves. However, as much as I relied on Maureen's, and everyone else's, greater experience in all things retail, instinctively this whole way of restocking the shelves just didn't feel right. Little consideration was rarely given to what was actually being sold, or if we had a run on something the previous day. Meaning that we often walked past part empty shelves whilst on our way to the next point on the schedule. I just felt that I needed to air this with someone who might be interested and wouldn't take it personally and sack me on the spot.

With Ross no longer at the shop, my go to person on the shop floor was Becky, the lady I briefly told you about before. The one that questioned Maureen's wise words relating to supermarkets. A feisty lady who'd been working at The Country Produce Store for about six months before I joined, so clearly had a lot more experience than me. She was, as I told you previously, also quite outspoken – about everything. Particularly the clunky nature of many of the things that went into the daily running of the place. Consequently, when I approached her about the replenishment programme, I unwittingly touched a nerve which opened the flood gates to a whole deluge of all the things that needed to be changed in the shop, including, but not limited to the whole management team. In fact, everything, and everyone, with the exception herself. I have no problem with anyone airing a view or two, but when riled Becky had only one volume setting and that was loud.

Meaning that she was drawing attention to us both. I decided to say nothing more hoping she would calm down a bit, which she did – eventually, although only to a simmering point. But being either inquisitive or stupid I continued. "I know I'm new to this game, but I'm thinking that it would make more sense to replenish the shop according to what the sales and stock system is telling us, don't you think?"

And so, the short fuse was reignited, and I really wanted the floor to open and swallow her up, as more of our colleagues started to take an interest. "Don't get me started on the stock system. In fact, it's not the stock system that's the problem it's the people, the management, the supervisors, the whole bloody lot of them!" With the assembled mob now nodding in agreement and getting uglier by the second – nothing implied. Just then, and as if things couldn't get any uglier, Denise arrived with a chuckle, asking us if everything was okay. With a supervisor now on the scene, albeit Denise, the mob quickly dispersed leaving me with Becky. But she decided against taking our conversation any further and moved on to no doubt rage at someone else – or the world in general.

It would seem that the stock system couldn't be relied upon. Hence why we did what we did. A disillusioned Becky was to leave within a few weeks and not be replaced. When I asked about any new replacement, I was advised, that in the first instance, it was none of my business and secondly management were monitoring the situation. In the meantime, the remaining shop floor team would need to close ranks and do what we could to provide cover.

In other words – do more.

I subsequently learnt that this method of 'closing ranks' isn't uncommon. Shop floor workers are often asked to take up the slack left by a leaving colleague, until such times as management deem that they have stretched the shop floor team far enough. Often to breaking point. Even at that point the decision to make any new appointment would rarely be in the interests of the welfare of the shop floor people. After all, up until that point the business had saved on a wage bill.

Thinking some more about stock replenishment brings to mind yet another unique type of customer behaviour.

It happened to me on numerous occasions when I was trying to fill a shelf, and someone wanted to get to where I was. Not a problem, after all the store is for their benefit not mine – another one of Gavin's straplines. Only here's how it often played out. "Are you going to be long?" with a huff or tut, being very typical opening gambits. I suspected much of this initial reaction was because I was in their way, meaning that they were going to have to engage with me, personally. At which point I would turn away from the shelf unit and switch on my most engaging smile. Within the safety of our home, I was to try out all manner of smiles with my wife where she considered, what I thought to be my 'engaging smile', the one I used most frequently, to be particularly creepy. In fact, she categorised all of my shop floor smiles as either creepy or maniacal. Going on to advise me that it might be best for everyone, not least of all any visiting children, if I didn't smile at all.

"I am indeed likely to be a long time, as I have the whole section to replenish, but let me move out of the way for you," and without further fuss or eye contact, I step aside. Some would thank me the majority not so. Another common antic is where the customer would reach across me and, in doing so, have no dialogue with me whatsoever. No "excuse me," no nothing. When this happened I would either offer to get whatever it was they were looking for, or, more often than not, say nothing, step aside and, contrary to Elaine's advice, making sure I smile at them as I do.

"Can't you do this kind of work at night? My supermarket does."

"No not really sir, because I'm usually tucked up in my bed at night."

* * *

Restocking the milk one morning I noticed a lady hovering. No not hovering, sorry that would be ridiculous, let's just say that she was loitering. "Are you looking for milk madam? Because I'm just about to put some out."

"I am, but you wouldn't catch me buying milk here, I only buy my milk at my [high end supermarket]."

I could have dropped the subject I guess and just got on with my day. But as these were still very early days for me on the shop floor, I was naively inclined to give people the benefit of any doubt, despite my instincts telling me otherwise. I would therefore offer to help. Even if the body language of the lady in question suggested that I would be impertinent to even try. "I understand madam, although I am told that the dairy that our milk comes from is also the same dairy that supplies [high end supermarket]."

For a while she just stared into the distance pondering the notion. Then turned to me and barked. "Don't be so ridiculous!"

And that was that. I stopped being ridiculous and got on with stocking the milk fridge.

* * *

Hardly having had any time to recover from being so ridiculous. "You don't seem to have any of those yoghurts that I like." Says a well-spoken, but gentle, elderly male voice. It belonged to a short, aged gentleman, who at some point in his life would have probably been much taller than he is now, had it not been for his head slowly sinking into his shoulders.

"And which yoghurts would they be sir?" As I turned to face the gentleman in question, tilting my head slightly to one side and putting my hand to my heart, trying to look as ingratiating as I could. A new look for me and on its first outing. Though instinctively knew I was failing when looking over the top of the enquiring man's head I spotted Sharon slowly shaking hers.

"The Fresh County Dairy ones from the dairy down the road."

"Ah yes sir, very popular. I know we had some in yesterday, but we appear to have sold them all. As they're made specially for us, we only have one weekly delivery. But what I can do if you like is to reserve some for you. We can even phone you when they're in if you prefer." I was on fire! Where was Maureen when I needed her? Although had she been in earshot I was in no doubt that she would have insisted that I go milk the cow, make the yoghurt, and deliver it to this gentleman's home. All by the end of the day.

"So, when is the next delivery?"

"That'll be next week sir, probably Tuesday."

"But how am I to know whether I'll want yoghurt next week? I know I'd like some now but as for next week I'm not so sure."

"So did you want me to reserve some for you or not sir?"

"I'm not sure, you've left me in a bit of a quandary if I'm being honest." And now it was his turn to shake his head as he turned away, leaving me feeling only slightly less ridiculous, but definitely an abject failure.

Useless fact for you - According to Dairy UK almost 15 billion litres of milk are produced each year. By my calculations that's enough to fill 6000 Olympic sized swimming pools. Or make 60 billion ice creams.

* * *

There's little doubt that the job of filling and refilling shelves can be a challenging although necessary one. But then if it wasn't for the antics of those few 'special' customers then it would have been quite a tedious one too. As for my colleagues, I know that few of them relished the job, but all do it to the best of their ability. Which goes for pretty much all the jobs that these people do, day in, day out. And let me add that they do all of this, and more, with a huge amount of pride. Regardless of the awkwardness of the customer. As for its often-clunky nature? Let's just say that like the steam engine it will be there long after the lights have gone out on the technology.

In spite of my initial reluctance to undertake shop floor work and some of the antics of the customers I was to nonetheless continue to enjoy my retail experience. One reason is that, compared to my former professional life, I didn't really need to think too much about stuff if I'm being perfectly honest. The Country Produce Store was an established hardly oiled machine, and I was just another rusty old cog happy to be a part of it. Or a 'bod' as someone once described my place within the business. I had few worries, largely I guess because I wasn't there to seek fame, fortune, or a career. After all, I'd already had a lengthy career in which someone was foolish enough to give me arguably too much authority, the personal consequence of which, was that I was perpetually tired – for years. Compared to my time at The Country Produce Store, where I had no authority whatsoever or any responsibility other than to do the job for which I was being paid to do. Which I can tell you is actually quite liberating. I could get in the car each evening, together with my back ache, and not have to think about work again until my next shift. The only exception being any lingering irritations, brought about mostly by The Entitled sorts. The ones that had done something or other to put a crease into my otherwise neat and tidy day. And, as much as I managed to bat most of them off with a quip or a condescending smile, there were still one or two that managed to get right under my thickening skin. Offset, I'm pleased to say, by the greater majority of customers, those that genuinely put a smile on my face – everyday.

SEVEN

MICHAEL, BOTTOM OF THE FOOD CHAIN, PERCEIVES
THE DRAMA OF MAKING TEA AND PARKING A CAR.

"Have you noticed how the shop front and carpark could do with a cleanup. Now the weathers a bit better would you like me to tackle that?" I had developed the knack of volunteering for jobs which actually didn't exist until I volunteered for them. The motive in this madness was largely to avoid stock replenishment as well as to get a bit of early Spring sunshine onto my face.

It was Denise, standing and staring out of the exit door for no apparent reason, that I was putting this idea (of hers) to. Immediately breaking into a chuckle. "Yes, I was just thinking the same thing to myself, good idea Mike [chuckle]. I'll get someone else to do the replen for the rest of the day if you'd like to crack on with that."

Mission accomplished.

Do you work here? – The shop floor chronicles

With both Ross and Becky now gone my next go to person on the shop floor for advice and knowledge was Sharon, the Irish lady who I made mention of before. She had been on the shop floor the longest of any of us (about two years) and is one of those people that everyone likes. She's dependable, polite to customers (most of the time), giving them the time of day no matter how busy we were, and did nothing beyond that set out in her job description. Although if there was such a thing as an actual 'job description' I never saw one in all the time I was there. But that never stopped Sharon referring to it.

Having successfully volunteered for the shop front and carpark cleaning job, which I extended to cleaning the few windows we had, I went and asked Sharon where I might find the broom, dusters, buckets and so on. "What do you want those for?"

"Because I've been asked by Denise to sweep the shop front, the carpark and clean the windows."

"Why you doing that? You wouldn't catch me doing that job."

"I guess, as I say, because I've been asked to do it and I'm learning not to ask questions."

Clearly not believing a word of it. "Nah, not for me, I don't come here to do that type of work. The broom, by the way, and everything else you'll probably need, is under the stairs out back." This was, if nothing else, a very typical response for anything that Sharon considered wasn't in *her* job description. Despite it being in everyone else's it would seem.

Which brings me nicely onto the subject of shop

floor politics. No matter where you go there is always workplace politics to contend with. Unwritten rules that determine pecking orders, hierarchies and a general way in which things are done outside of the officialdom of management. The Country Produce Store was no exception. Although I had been working at the shop for just under three months now, I was still considered as the newbie and therefore bottom of the food chain in the eyes of everyone, on and off of the shop floor. Until the store finally relented and employed a new lad, I was the person that did as he was told, by everyone; I made the tea twice a day for everyone, I was expected to do the not so glamourous daily jobs, not that any of them were particularly glamorous, and I was regularly called upon to fetch and carry. Mainly because I was the only bloke on the shop floor most of the time and therefore tradition, or my sex, dictated, that I do lift and shift. Regardless of the fact that I was no bigger in stature than one or two of the shop floor ladies. But I have an unwritten rule, and that is, 'don't moan'. There's little point and no one likes a moaner. This was equally true on the shop floor because everyone has their own things to deal with, both in and outside of the shop. Ultimately if you don't like the job then either lump it or leave.

As I told you previously, my only notable, and, as it turned out, serious transgression to date was to give someone their tea in the wrong mug. Do it once, to anyone, and you're just plain useless. Do it more than once and there'd be a clamour for you to be sacked. I'm exaggerating of course. But as much as it seemed as though I could get away with practically anything, tea in the wrong mug was literally unforgivable.

It was strange though, being considered as the newbie, that is. Which got me thinking about how it must be for all those other people, of a similar age to me, going back into the workplace. Particularly into jobs for which they have no previous experience. Reading various news items recently I saw a lot about how people over 55, or those recently retired, are being encouraged to go back into the workplace. Surprisingly none of these articles were written by my wife by the way. These people are being asked to fill staffing shortages in sectors such as hospitality and retail. With most vacancies typically being, in the case of hospitality, waiting staff, and in retail, shop floor staff. Which is all well and good if you're able; and should you have the inclination to do so then I say, "go for it." But from my own personal experience let me tell you that the actual transition can be quite something. Not only are you having to take on board all that goes with being in a new working environment, or in my case, a completely alien one, but there is also living with a reality that any previous professional status that you may have had, accounts for bugger all. At The Country Produce Store, I was now very much a bod sitting at the bottom of the food chain. My opinions and business acumen were of little interest to my bosses who wanted nothing more than for me to do my job in the manner in which they prescribed. I guess the point I'm trying to make is that if you decide to go back into the workplace, particularly into the type of job such as I did, then there are three things that I strongly advise you to do. Swallow your pride, always respect your bosses' position, and do whatever you're asked to the best of your ability. If you're unable to do any of those things, then stay at home.

* * *

Back to the job of tidying up the shop front.

It was such a lovely day, so I was in no hurry to go back inside, meaning that each and every window received my utmost attention. As indeed did the rest of the shop front and the carpark. Even the small ads board, the one on which I was proposing to post a card re the lost (dead) cat, got a tidy up. With old notices being removed and others being reordered to give the whole a more professional look about it. The noticeboard seemed to be a popular space for locals to advertise events as well as things for sale. During my time at the shop, I was asked to post many such adverts. Most banal, although some I'm pleased to report, unintentionally funny. Which I'll share as we go. For example:

EXPERIENCED LADY GARDENER, AVAILABLE NOW. PLEASE CALL, [phone number]

But nothing more would happen until I'd had my lunch. With the weather providing an opportunity for me not to have to use the staff restroom and avoiding being an agony aunt to Gavin's IT problems, I decided to take up residence on one of the wooden picnic benches outside of the coffee shop. Unpacking my homemade cheese roll and with the sun on my back I planned to just sit and watch the world go by. Or at least the world within the boundary of The

Country Produce Store. On another bench sat an oldish pair whose conversation I couldn't help overhearing. Their patois suggested that they were a couple of local blokes who I am sure I'd seen in our local pub once or twice. With one of them having a large but lovely, impeccably behaved, dog laying at his feet.

"That dog new then?"

"No, ad im for a couple o months now. Bought im from a bloke in the arrers." The arrers being the Quiver of Arrows pub. The local I was just referring to.

"E's a gooden by the looks of im."

"Yeah, good as gold. Pedigree e is, so the bloke in the pub told me. E's got the papers somewhere, an e's goin to let me av em. If wot he says is true I'm thinkin of showin im."

Then there's a pause, a really long pause.

"Showin im what?"

* * *

Leisurely sweeping and doing some much-needed litter picking gave me time to observe the antics of the people coming in to park their cars. If you happen to have a few spare minutes the next time you're out shopping, I urge you to stop and look at how people behave, particularly in the carpark. And this day's performers didn't disappoint.

Ranging from the lazy sods that simply abandon their trolleys, to the arguably more interesting which are the car owners themselves.

But first let me share with you a couple of examples of carpark behaviour, by way of a general observation. Have you ever noticed how it is often too much trouble for new arrivals to the carpark to stop and let someone reverse out of a space. When it would be easier than doing what they inevitably do, and that is to slalom around the exiting car, causing it to make an emergency stop as its arse is part way out. Another is the need for some people to get as close to the entrance to the shop as possible. Irrespective of how many other vacant parking spaces there are, these types would rather shout out of their window to the person currently occupying a prime spot close to the shop door. "Are you going to be long?" It would seem that anything under ten minutes is acceptable as they choose to sit and wait. In doing so, watching the current carparking space occupants unload their shopping from trolley to car until they finally drive away. In the meantime, they are blissfully ignorant of the gridlock behind them. Extremely satisfied with themselves for saving a few yards of walking, they pull into the now vacant space. It never seems to occur to these people, that had they opted to park elsewhere they would have probably been in the shop already.

More specifically to my day tidying the front of the shop, I was blessed to witness a particular favourite of mine, the classic marshalling a car into a space. Usually undertaken exclusively by senior citizens, and today was no exception. A smallish German made hatchback approached a vacant space between two already parked cars, and the passenger, an older gent, sprang from the car. This, I'm thinking, would be the self-appointed Marshal. Leaping round to the front and instantly shouting instructions to the driver, who I took to be his wife, seemingly already anxious by what was about to occur. Probably because she'd been through the same nightmare many times before. The first thing he does is to mime the act of winding down a car window. A cranking motion in the old-fashioned way as if he were actually winding a handle – despite the fact that the windows were likely electric. Anyway, she got the message because both driver and passenger windows duly opened. Then the real fun started. Waving his arms in a windmill fashion, akin to moving a very large imaginary steering wheel. "Right love left hand down!" and slowly the wheels turned in the opposite direction to which they were supposed to. "No love, the other way, I said left hand down!"

"But I don't know what that means, I never know what that means!" Look in the dictionary for the word 'pleading' and I'm pretty sure you'll find this poor woman's picture.

Unmoved by his wife's pleas, and her continued look of confusion, he resumes with his frenetic gesticulating. Eventually the car is in the space. But it would seem that the gap between their car and the two either side isn't the same. Resulting in the poor woman having to manoeuvre the car in and out of the parking space numerous times, before it is deemed, by the Marshal, to be satisfactorily lined up. He then literally runs around to the back of the car. And using both hands, whilst crouching down so they can lock eyes, her in the mirror and him through the back window, he waves her back until he's satisfied with the gap at the rear. Once the car is deemed to be in the right position the tailgate receives a resounding smack from the Marshal followed instantly by a shout. "Stop! That'll do love!" In the meantime, there's gridlock. To be honest I wasn't sure as to whether some polite applause would be appropriate, but thought better of it, seeing the bloke's wife sitting bolt upright and petrified. Clearly with no intention of getting out of the car anytime soon.

Meanwhile the husband, as if nothing had just happened. "You getting out love? Can't sit there all day you know."

"Just give me a moment, will you?" she sighs.

Another one for you, which you yourself may have been the victim or perpetrator of. I refer to those people that take up more than one space, possibly because they do not want someone parking next to them, or they just can't drive properly, or they don't give a damn, or maybe all three. Added to that there are the ones that park so close to an adjacent car that the returning owners struggle to get into their car.

When you get both of these types in play at the same time it is the perfect storm (or pantomime) to the casual onlooker. As I was lucky enough to be whilst doing the last of my outdoor jobs – emptying the perimeter bins.

It all started when a youngish couple decided to park their very new German SUV into a space and a half. Looking at it I found myself thinking, how is it that such cars are often the vehicle of choice for school runs? And despite its capabilities you will rarely see one 'off road'. A few minutes later, while my back was turned, a small Japanese city car had managed to park in the available half space. In doing so leaving a gap of no more than a few inches between its passenger side and the SUV driver's door. Although being sure to leave plenty of space on the driver's side of the Japanese city car for the elderly lady owner to be able to open her door fully and climb out. Then a man in a van came along and cleverly reversed into the space on the other side of the SUV. In doing so leaving a decent enough space on both of his sides. Curious as to how this might play out my bin emptying duties slowed considerably. As it happened I didn't have to wait too long as the youngish upwardly mobile couple came back to their car carrying quite a few bags full of produce. In doing so they immediately saw the challenge presented to them, and upon seeing me the youngish man beckoned me across in a well-spoken voice and a, 'I always get my own way' type of manner. "Can you come here, please?" I did as he asked, and in doing so tried to look as surprised as they clearly were, changing quickly to my best sympathetic look – I have no idea what that looks like in reality. "Oh my that looks awkward, how can I help?"

It was now the youngish lady's turn to speak up, also in a well-spoken voice and an equally, 'I always get my own way' type of manner. "We can't get into our car; can you go find the owner of *that* little car – condescendingly pointing at the Japanese city car – and get them to move it, so that my husband can get into the driver's side?"

"I have no idea who the owners are madam, but what I can do is to call the registration number of the car into the shop using my radio and get some of my colleagues to ask around for you. Unfortunately, we don't have a public address system, so that's the best I can do I'm afraid." Adding a shrug for no particular reason.

Without further acknowledgement of my existence and clearly not in any mood to wait, they proceeded to load their shopping into the boot of their car, and I radioed into the shop. Whilst doing so, I could hear them discussing the possibility of how one of them could get into the passenger side and crawl across the centre console and onto the driver's seat. With them both agreeing that this was their best and only course of action and clearly a man's job, the youngish man proceeded to do just that. With grunting, cussing, admirable agility, and a small crowd forming he achieved his goal in surprisingly quick time. Clearly agitated at the attention he was attracting he shouted a proposal to his wife. "Would you mind getting into the fucking car!" She obligingly stepped up and into the car but as she did so offered her husband her own piece of advice. "Don't you dare fucking swear at me!" He then gunned the engine, reversed out of their one and a half spaces, and left us in silence. I turned to the gathered audience, shrugged once more, and moved off to finish my chores. It was then that I heard one of our fascinated onlookers, an older lady who I'd seen earlier – the Japanese city car owner – say to no one in particular. "Well that was a bit of a palaver wasn't it? If they'd asked, I would have moved my car out of the way for them. Some people, eh?" And with that, she placed her shopping and herself into her little car and serenely drove away.

The radio then buzzed into life. "Mike, sorry but we can't find the owner of the car you were looking for."

"No worries, all sorted out here, thanks."

"Mike, it's very dry in here, could you please come in and make the tea, thanks."

* * *

Finally, whilst I'm on the subject of shop car parks I'd like to touch on the subject of dogs that are left in hot cars. There is so much evidence and advice telling all dog (and cat) owners that it's a bad thing to do. But still people do it. During the summer months we were extra vigilant and had posters around the shop in an effort to raise people's awareness. I also see that the RSPCA run campaigns on popular social media platforms, #DogsDieInHotCars.

I know it's common practise for many people to pop into the shops on the way to or from a dog walk or indeed take their dogs with them on holiday. We've done the same many a time. Though none of which can be offered as an excuse for putting your dog's life at risk.

I remember on one particularly warm day when an observant customer came into the shop telling us that they'd seen a dog left in a car and gave us the registration number hoping we could track down the owners. If you recall from the car parking incident I was just telling you about, there is no public address system available to us. So, our only option was to walk the shop progressively asking each customer whether they owned the car in question. The owners, on this occasion, a family of five – mum, dad and three young children – were finally found, and the situation explained to them. The thing that struck me as I was talking to them was that they seemed genuinely put out that one or other would have to break off from shopping to go attend to their dog. For my part I offered a bowl of water for the dog, which was ungratefully received by the dad as he took it from me and proceeded to walk back out to the carpark. But here's the rub, as he got to the exit he turned to me. "You do realise that we wouldn't have had to have left the dog in the car if you allowed dogs into the shop."

I was no longer astounded by the behaviour of a significant number of our customers, but I was quickly learning the futility of arguing a point to people that have no sense of reason. So, I chose, in this case, to just shrug, smile, and get on with whatever job I'd been doing.

I'm pleased to say that dogs locked in hot cars was a rare thing for us and on most occasions when people were advised of the fact, they seemed genuinely remorseful. Some even thanked us.

A bit of related information for you before we move on.

Apparently it's not illegal to leave a pet unattended in a car in the UK. However, if the animal becomes ill or dies due to being left, you can be charged with animal cruelty under the Animal Welfare Act 2006. In such cases, you can be sentenced to up to 51 weeks in jail and hit with a fine of up to £20,000. All of which is a good thing.

However, having trawled the Web for quite a while I was to find not one case where a maximum fine or jail sentence had been handed out to offenders.

EIGHT

TROUBLE, TROUBLEMAKER, TROUBLESOME,
TROUBLER, TROUBLESOMELY, TROUBLESOMENESS,
FOR THE RETICENT MAN.

"Do we have any anchovy paste on the shelf Mike?" was the latest radio message I received as I assuredly walked the shop floor that, having now been here for the best part of five months, I was a lifer of. I was also soon to no longer be the newbie because a new lad, Bramble, had agreed to start in a few weeks' time. More about him later.

With my heightened knowledge of all things retail and tolerance levels increasingly fragile I was slowly, but surely, becoming the model inmate. Perfectly adjusted for life in The Country Produce Store. So much so that I was frequently finding myself being the first point of contact on the two-way radio. Being asked all manner of obscure things which only a seasoned internee such as myself would be able to answer. I would confidently reply to such enquiries, with all the false bravado that a convict needs as he calmly walks around the exercise yard. Hoping that parole would be somewhere on the horizon.

Sadly, not only did I now know what anchovy paste was, but I knew exactly where it could be found and if we had any on the shelf. "No, we don't," I confidently fired back. And for no particular reason, I took the opportunity to do a bit of unnecessary showboating. "But we do have both tinned and chilled anchovies."

To which the reply came back. "Yeah thanks Mike, that's great, if someone comes in asking for tinned or chilled anchovies, I'll send them straight to you." Sarcasm is one of the many ways that the people on the shop floor, me included, got through the day, most often at someone else's expense.

* * *

"Excuse me mate, can I put a card in your noticeboard out front?" I turned to see a burly bloke handing me a handwritten postcard.

"Sure thing," proceeding to read it through to make sure it complied with shop rules, of which there were few. Lines seemed to be drawn at selling guns, sexual favours, and elderly relatives.

Septic tank emptying and repairs. Toilets and drains unblocked – We can tackle big jobs and small jobs. Tel Jake.

"You sure this is how you want it to read?"

"That's what we do, so yeah."

"Okay that'll be fifty pence for the month please."

* * *

Doing my daily fruit and veg inspection one morning, picking through an assortment of old men's penises – or penii as the Greeks might say – I glimpsed a gentleman lurking a few yards away, clearly seeking mine or someone else's attention. Knowing that I needed to get this job done before the shop became too busy and the fact that there were quite a few of my colleagues on the shop floor, I chose to ignore him. However, to gain my attention he started to sidle up to me, getting ever closer to the point where it became impossible for me to ignore him any longer.

Stupid question number one of the day went to the lurking man. No prize though, just a sigh and a smile from me. "Excuse me, are you busy?"

Looking up at him from my crouching position and thinking and almost being inclined to say; "Nope I always place my face near to and fondle the cucumbers, apparently they're good for your skin." Actually, now I come to think about it I often did place my face close to all manner of fruit and vegetables. In doing so fondly remembering Ross's induction in the art of produce inspection. Then instantly forgetting it, as the thought of 'old man's genitalia' and 'close to my face' were not words that I wanted to hear or use in the same sentence.

"Not at all sir, how may I help you?" Then I notice the shopping list in his hand. Oh, Christ I hoped he hadn't been sent out shopping by your wife. Why? Because he'll have no idea where anything is, and he likely won't have the inclination, like most normal shoppers, to simply peruse the shelves to find what he's been sent out to buy. Especially with me being on hand. I'd had this a few times now and in each case, I would end up being someone's – mostly blokes – personal shopper.

"My wife has asked me to grab a few things, can you tell me where I might find the eggs?" And there it is! Proffering me the little note that no doubt his wife had written for him. Falling short of tucking it into his glove along with the money, "to give to the nice man". Standing in front of me I was reminded of a little schoolboy giving over a letter from his mum, explaining that little Charlie needed to be excused sports today, and every other day, because he was too frail to be outside in the weather – any weather.

"Yes sir, eggs you say? That's easy, just behind you." Although he didn't turn to select some eggs he simply moved on to the next thing on the list, that I'd chosen *not* to take from him. This went on for the next three or four items and each time he simply looked across at where I pointed to in the shop. And neither of us moved. This was a classic Mexican standoff, but with groceries replacing guns or knives and with barely a hint of aggression – yet. Then at line item five he gave me the opportunity I was looking for.

"Would you recommend prepacked or fresh sausages?"

Hah, got you! "Fresh every time sir, let me take you across to the butchery counter." And off we went. Or rather off we went with me persuasively leading him, having attached myself with thumb and forefinger to his raincoat sleeve.

Although when I returned to continue with my fruit and veg, I noticed that he had left his trolley behind. A smart move indeed because he still had me 'in-play'. Then the most wonderful thing happened. From behind the bought in homemade cake stand, Sharon appeared. I swear at that moment I had never been so happy to see her. Now I come to think of it I can't recall a time when I would have been happy to see her. But there you have it, needs must, I guess. Not that there was anything particularly wrong with Sharon she was just a bit dour that's all. Or maybe that was just for my benefit?

Anyway, seizing the opportunity. "Here you are sir here's your trolley, that'll save your legs, oh and this is Sharon by the way, have you met Sharon? She's been here for ages and knows where practically everything is. You have yourself a great day."

Introductions made I quickly retreated to bury my face back into the cucumbers.

Being an old hand Sharon knew exactly what I was up to as she gave me one of those 'Don't you worry, I know where you live' kind of looks. And in doing so sending a clear message that said, 'if you think I'm being dour now you ain't seen nothing yet.'

* * *

Having shaken off 'Lurking Gent' I needed to get my head down and finish checking and replenishing the fruit and veg but not before Maureen came along with one of her classics. "Everything okay Michael?"

Yet another of those impossible to answer questions. "Yes" and she'd likely add, "Well I only ask because that job seems to be taking you a long time?" Or "No" and I'd get a summons, "Well come and see me after you've finished that job, which does seem to be taking you a long time?" I opted for a 'yes' which seemed to temporarily satisfy her curiosity.

After a short while I was to notice a presence once again. This time more of a shadow. Briefly looking up I saw an older sun-dried lady staring down at me. No, she was more than that. Here was a lady who had probably, in the 1960's and well into her thirties at the time, determined that she quite liked the hippie look and so deciding that these were the clothes and hairstyle for her – forever! Standing alongside her was an equally sun-dried gentleman who had clearly followed her lead. Although in his case he'd added a ponytail to his now grey receding hairline, multiple ear and nose piercings and deciding during those heady 'make love, not war' times that bathing wasn't for him. Perceptively deduced because I was kneeling downwind of him.

"Are your fruit and vegetables organic?" Hippy lady asked. It would seem that despite her having a spiritual nature and being a groovy daughter of flowers, didn't extend to her possessing common courtesies such as a good morning.

Over the years I've learnt to spot a troublemaker a mile off and I can tell you that they come in all shapes and sizes. And here was a troublemaker in the form of an old hippie and her hippie mate in the form of a scarecrow needing a damn good scrub. I had to think fast, and in doing so concluded that there was only one answer that I could realistically give to these people if I wanted to avoid further interrogation. To respond otherwise I would no doubt find myself being the subject of unwanted attention. Across the way, still trying to manoeuvre herself away from 'Lurking Gent' I saw Sharon looking across at me. And there on her face in all its smug glory was a look of absolute triumph.

Standing up and turning slightly so as to move out of Sharon's eyeline, I did a theatrical sweeping gesture with my arm across the fruit and vegetable display and declared. "Absolutely madam, all organic, everything." And with that she just turned and walked off, closely followed by her (pri)mate. No further enquiry no thanks for your time, just the sound of old leather soled feet on the not quite so old wooden floor. Keeping an eye on them just in case they'd considered my answer and found it to be wanting, I noticed that neither of them actually bought anything as they continued on through the store and towards the exit. But not before stopping at the fresh fish counter, adjacent to the butchery – which I'll come back to later – to ask Gary a question. "Is your salmon farmed?" to which the reply from young Gary was outstanding. "Absolutely not madam, but all our meat is if you're interested." It would seem as though I wasn't the only one at The Country Produce Store that had learnt that the right answer to a troublemaker's question is always the one they are wanting to hear. But in doing so being sure to avoid telling an outright lie. Seemingly satisfied, and not savvy enough to catch Gary's little jibe, they left the building.

Curious as to what sort of love machine our cliché hippies had arrived in, I stopped what I was doing and sneaked a peak out of the door. Only to see them drive off in a battered old Skoda. Leaving me to think that maybe they were friends of Gavin's?

Sharon seeing of all this unfold detached herself from Lurking Gent and walked over to me. "Did I just hear you tell a lie to those customers?"

"For start they weren't customers because they never actually bought anything and as for telling them a lie – absolutely not. I think you'll find that all of our fruit and vegetables are in fact organic."

"No, they're not!" Clearly, she had no intention of letting me off the hook that I'd conveniently swallowed for her.

"Okay," I said, "let me ask you a question. Are any of our fruit or vegetables made from, plastic, metal, glass or any other such materials?"

"No of course not."

"In which case they must all be organic then." Followed up with what I hoped was my best self-satisfied smile. She in turn gave me the classic middle finger salute and headed away, being careful to avoid 'Lurking Gent', who was now in the character-building situation of having to fend for himself. Tenuous I know and probably wouldn't stand up to scrutiny if the Soil Association were to pay us a visit any time soon. But then the alternative would have no doubt been a long and tedious debate with Mr and Mrs Tattie-bogle.

In case you're thinking of taking me to task as Sharon had unsuccessfully tried to do.

Definition of Organic - *relating to or derived from living matter* – Get in there!

And for your further education.

Tattie-bogle – *Something akin to a scarecrow usually made out of sticks and old clothes to scare birds away from crops. Or in Scotland a scarecrow in a potato field with 'tattie' being a common term for potato.*

* * *

But The Country Produce Store, or should I say the countryside in general; the thought of living here, maybe off-grid, is considered by some as an idyll. Often attracting aspiring artists from the city. And if we were in any doubt as to who or what they were, then they would tell us as much when they came into the shop, dressed as they often are, in some kind of smock or ill-fitting shirt and pullover. All of which would be sporting copious amounts of paint, plaster, bits of twig... Some would often ask if they could display or sell their pictures in the shop, which Angela never agreed to. Explaining to them that we didn't have the space as there was little enough room for all the other goods on offer. But we suspected that was only half the truth.

To curry favour before asking for a manager one or two would ask for our, the shop floor workers, opinion on a piece of artwork. Not being used to having an opinion we struggled somewhat, and so politely declined. But artists, in my humble opinion, are a peculiar species. Many that I met possessed quite a narrow view on the world and therefore, I'm delighted to say, were wonderfully oblivious to shop floor humour and irony. So much so that on one occasion I heard a curious Sharon speaking with a bearded gentleman, sporting a wide brimmed hat and the mandatory baggy pullover. "Excuse me can I ask you a question?"

"Of course, my dear, fire away."

"I'm wondering, does being a painter mean that you have to spill a lot of paint on yourself?"

"I'm sorry I don't understand."

"It's just that you all seem to have more paint on your clothes than you do on the paintings you create, that's all. My husbands a painter, and he doesn't get half the paint on him that you lot seem to."

"Oh he is, is he? What's his specialism, oils, watercolour, pastel?"

"Ceilings and walls mostly. Inside or out he's not fussed. He also sometimes turns his hand to wallpapering but it's not his thing really."

Now that was a picture worth painting. The look on that man's face I mean.

* * *

Back to the fish counter for a moment. All the fresh fish at The Country Produce Store is displayed on a bed of ice. There isn't much on offer because after all this is a farm shop, but there does seem to be a demand for such produce, albeit limited. Anyway, at some point during the time of 'Lurking Gent' and the Tattie-bogles a bloke had come in and bought some fish. Sorry I can't be more specific as to what type of fish, because I'm telling this to you third hand via one of Pete the butcher's other lads. The following day a phone call comes in from this same bloke claiming that our fish gave him 'gut rot'. Again, not my words but the lads. Pete spoke to the fella in question, sympathised for his predicament and as good manners dictate offered an apology. But an apology wasn't going to cut it so Pete offered him a full refund, despite the fact that his 'gut rot' could have been anything other than the fish. As a point of interest Pete asked the fella whether the fish had been put in the fridge when he got home and before he cooked and ate it. To which the fella replied. "No I left it wrapped on the side in our kitchen. No one told me to put it in the fridge so you can't hang that one on me. And yes, I would like a refund, and no I won't be buying fish from you ever again."

"But I think you'll find sir that the label on the packet in which the fish was wrapped, clearly states that the fish should be kept refrigerated, as well as telling you within what period it should be consumed."

"That may be the case, but no one told me. I'll be in for my refund later."

This fish story is just one of many examples that have been shared with me, where disgruntled and immoral people find shops an easy target to make trouble with. In most shops you'll find that it is policy for staff not to argue with customers regardless of the grievance – justifiable or otherwise. Making them, as I say, an easy target, which is all too often taken advantage of by the wrong sorts.

Do you work here? – The shop floor chronicles

Something that I believe is also one of the many reasons why shoplifters are in the ascendancy in the UK. A subject I will touch on later.

But I would like to offer a quiet word in the ear of all you troublemakers out there; If you're going to ask a question, especially to someone like me – please be specific. Alternatively, if it's a question where you are somehow looking to make an assertion, score points or boost your own sense of self-worth then don't. Because despite how clever you think you are being, believe me when I tell you that as soon as you open your mouth the games up. You've revealed yourself to be an arse.

Let me give you an example.

One day a fella asked me what the typical shelf life of our fresh herbs was. Not knowing and being honest about the fact, I told him as much. Although adding that I could find out for him. But of course, he already knew the answer, which he was only too eager to share. Going on to reveal that he grew and provided herbs to some restaurant or other. All he got for his poor attempt at showing off was the best condescending smile I could muster and me telling him. "You must be very proud of yourself sir." Not getting at all the double entendre in that very simple sentence. I rest my case.

This had me thinking that shops ought to have a 'troublemaker zone', much like the 'quiet zone' on a train. With a sign, situated at the entrance to the shop, guiding them towards the area, reading something along the lines of: If you are inclined towards being troublesome then please make your way to our 'troublemaker zone', where no-one will be in attendance for quite some time.

* * *

Over the course of my time at The Country Produce Store there were numerous instances of challenges, and verbal scuffles with The Entitled, and one or two run ins with quite a few others, who just seemed to be confused.

With the fruit and vegetables being in such a prominent position, meant that I was often the first point of contact for quite a few of the nutters and self-proclaimed experts that passed through our doors.

One morning I was doing my thing when one such person came up to me, wearing what I instantly recognised as being a condescending smirk. "I'm sure it's nothing to do with you, but can I ask why you are selling Spanish plums in a shop that makes numerous claims about providing and producing locally sourced food?"

My initial thoughts were – Oh God not another one, closely followed up with wondering whether there was enough room in the aisle for me to perform a drop kick. But, most of all, I'm thinking that they really need to give someone else a go at this job by the door. Do people really have nothing better to do with their time? But then I switched seamlessly into helpful mode, complete with my own unique style of smile, that said; I'll answer your question a lot more politely than your tone deserved.

"Well madam the simple answer to your question is that I don't know. However, if I were to speculate

I would say that there seems to be a demand for certain soft fruits to be available all year round. Particularly in this country." Then after taking a short breath, and holding my smile firmly in place, I continued. "Therefore, by selling Spanish plums at this time of the year, we're merely satisfying that demand. But let me add that you were right in what you said in the first place." At which point she beamed a rather unnecessary 'I told you so' smile. But fading instantly as I continued. "It is absolutely nothing whatsoever to do with me. Anything else I can help you with today madam?" Leaving at least one of us still smiling.

* * *

And the day rolls on.

"Tell me young man can I ask you to have a word with your manager?"

The young man reference I had no problem with, but as for the abrupt intro….. "Certainly, madam and what is it that you'd like me to say to her?"

"Would it be possible for you to get all the weights on the labels for the fruit and vegetables changed to pounds and ounces, I get really confused you see. I mean what is a kilogram anyway?"

"Absolutely, let me see what I can do for you madam, leave it with me."

A bit of context for you if you didn't already know; *The UK started its transition to metric in the mid to late 1960's. By the end of the 1970's metric weights were commonplace in shops and by 1995 (nearly 30 years ago) metrification was complete and in law.*

I did in fact run this customer enquiry past Angela, and I am sure that you will not be surprised to hear that she did nothing. And why would she? Although believe it or not and despite my dismissive attitude to this lady's dilemma, I do sympathise with how elderly people might struggle with the pace of change in society today, as indeed I do at times. Though maybe not so much regarding changes that have been a part of our lives for more than half the time I've been on the planet. There comes a point at which you need to accept that this change, and many like it, are here to stay, therefore leaving you with little alternative other than to fall in line. Alright you still get beer in pints and golf courses in yards, but that's beside the point and perfectly okay in my 'little book of self-serving needs'.

That is because I know exactly where I am when I have a pint of beer in my hand or standing alongside the 100-yard marker on a golf course. Nowhere near The Country Produce Store and having to field ridiculous questions.

I was in our local supermarket recently and saw how they'd issued tee shirts to some of the poor buggers on the shop floor, adorned with big white letters stating that they are 'Happy to help' or 'I'm Here for You' or some other such slogan. I have no objection to this whatsoever, although how about an alternative slogan? 'I'm happy to help' on the back, and then on the front, 'Unless you're a moron'.

* * *

Another confused soul for you.

A lady was proffering a roll of prepacked butter in my direction. "Can I ask you a question about your butter?"

I wouldn't claim to be an authority on butter, but I was still willing to give it my best shot. "Of course, madam, fire away."

"Why do you make the butter too big to fit into my butter dish? I put the butter in the dish, put its lid on and when I lift it off again there's butter smeared on the underside of the lid."

Well, I never saw that coming, and for a long moment I was stumped for an answer. Sarcastic or otherwise. Seeing that she was deadly serious I opted for an otherwise answer. "Could it be that the fault lies, not with the butter, but in the size of your butter dish?"

To give her some due she didn't dismiss my suggestion out of hand, although from the look on her face I wasn't expecting her to agree either. "No that can't be right, I've had the same butter dish for years."

Maybe she had a point, or I was having to deal, once again, with the imperial (pounds and ounces) versus metric measure thing, and the block of butter was bigger than it used to be? Although I was pretty sure it was the same standard weight and size you would find in any supermarket anywhere in the land. To conclude the conversation in the best way I knew, I simply shrugged, apologised, and carried on loading more oversized butter into the cold cabinet. She in turn also shrugged and put the pack of butter into her basket and moved on, with both her life and shopping.

Make of that what you will.

NINE

A STARTLED RABBIT IN THE FORM OF A YOUNG MAN
STEPS INTO THE HEADLIGHTS.

"Mike, this is our new team member." This was Maureen introducing me to the new lad, Bramble, who, with typical teenage awkwardness, was trying to blend in with the wall.

"So not my replacement then?"

"You don't get off the hook that easy Mike. No, he's spending some time with us before he goes off to college in September."

College? Surely not, the lad couldn't have been more than twelve years old. Though to him I was probably prehistoric. "College you say?"

Before Bramble could confirm as much Maureen was on it in a flash. "Yes Michael and don't say another word." She knew exactly what I was thinking. Probably because she was thinking the same herself. I also knew she was getting serious because she called me Michael, so decided instead to say nothing more. "So, Bramble for this morning I'd like you to shadow Mike and then after lunch we'll put you with someone who actually knows a thing or two."

But something was off, which I couldn't quite put my finger on, so I lingered. Bramble stood stock still, bemused by what was, or rather wasn't happening, and Maureen, equally as puzzled, just stared at me. Almost willing me to move. Then the penny dropped. "Oh, and don't forget your radio. Don't let me catch either of you – moving her steely gaze from one to the other – on the shop floor without your radio, we need to be able to always contact you. Any questions? – No? Good. Off you go then." And there it was, the missing radio speech. Normal business had been resumed. And no, she still didn't go on and tell us to, "Stay safe out there."

We were stopped at the door however, by Gavin. "Ah, is this new blood I see amongst us, hello young man, pleased to meet you." Despite the fact that he had interviewed the lad only a week or two before. Maureen chose to raise her eyes to the sky, perhaps looking for some divine intervention of the lightning bolt kind but receiving none. Whilst I rocked back and forth, heels to toes, and waited for his trademark random question. "I'm thinking that the stockroom could do with a lick of paint, what do you think?" That man never failed to deliver.

"What to paint over the cracks you mean?" offered Maureen. Then turning away, calling time on any further interaction with someone who she clearly had little time for. I, in turn, grabbed a couple of radios from the wall charger, and took the scared rabbit out of the headlights and on to the shop floor. Gavin, with his audience gone, went back to his office, I assumed to check out paint colours.

"So, Bramble we'll start with some of the regular morning jobs, and you can tell me all about yourself, your ambitions and why your parents chose to give you such an absurd name."

As it turned out, I wasn't to spend much time with the lad, because as Maureen suggested his time was better spent working alongside people that knew a thing or two about retail. But I liked Bramble – straightaway. Especially after my initial barrage of what must have sounded like boorish interview questions. All of which he politely answered, bar the one about his name. He chose to deal with that one separately, and as it turned out, perfectly. "As for my name I know it's ridiculous, but I'm stuck with it, so can we please shut the fuck up about it?"

"Absolutely!" And as we both laughed, I handed the newbie bod a box of toilet rolls, a gallon container of hand soap and instructed him to go check out the state of play in the staff restroom, the customer toilet in the coffee shop, and restock each of them, as necessary.

Each morning, throughout the day and in the evening, there was a schedule of daily tasks. The list was systematically worked through by the shop floor team. None of them were particularly glamorous, but all necessary. They included: emptying the bins (shop floor, stockroom, tearoom, toilets) washing up, litter picking outside (regardless of the weather), refilling soap and toilet rolls and so on.

* * *

The fruit and vegetables were being sorted by Sharon, so Bramble was spared Ross's inspection guide, which, you may be surprised to hear, I continued to use right up to the time I left the shop. Leading me to ponder, as to what Sharon's method or categorisation was. So, I asked.

"Morning Sharon, this is Bramble he's joined us today."

"What and they put him with you? I'd think about placing a bet that he won't last the day, but the odds are probably already low." What is it about the Irish accent that makes a sarcastic phrase sound almost conversational?

Choosing to ignore the barb. "Before Ross left, he showed me a pretty good way of categorising the fruit and veg, which I still find useful. I've never thought to ask but what method do you use. If indeed you use one at all?"

"What you mean the old man's penis and scrotum thing?" Hearing Sharon saying penis and scrotum seemed to cause Bramble to blink rapidly and take two involuntary steps backwards. Which I noticed, but Sharon seemed not to. "Yeah of course I've heard it. What is it with you blokes? It's all penis this and breasts that. You need help, the lot of you!"

"Ok so what method do you use, if any?"

"This might come as a surprise to you Michael, but I don't need and don't have a method, as you put it, for categorising vegetables. When I see a dodgy courgette or cucumber – picking one up and waving it around in case we didn't know what a courgette looked like – I simply think, mmm, there's a dodgy courgette or cucumber, I think I need to take that somewhere and do something with it." The startled rabbit was firmly back in the headlights, and I was nodding sagely at Sharon, whilst trying to supress a boyish titter.

But I couldn't let it slide. "To be honest with you Sharon I'm not sure that's any less dubious than Ross's approach. And as for the soft fruit I suggest that you keep that to yourself."

"What are you talking about!" Then a pause for reflection. "Oh for fucks sake, really! You need help, both of you, bugger off the pair of you!"

Leaving Sharon, but feeling her eyes burning into our backs, I took the lad to the coffee shop to meet the Ali's, purposefully avoiding the butchery. I needed to work up to that one.

"Morning Mike, are you upsetting Sharon again?"

"You don't want to know. So, this is Bramble, and Bramble this is our Ginger Ali. No not our Ginger Ali, but the Ginger Ali that works here in the Coffee shop. As opposed to Skinny Ali, who also works in the coffee shop." I'm pretty sure I could have done that a lot better, but luckily, as if on cue, Skinny Ali appeared from the toilet.

"Morning Mike, are you upsetting Sharon again?"

"What you heard all that from inside the toilet?"

"You'd be amazed what can be heard going on

from either side of that door."

"Either side of the door you say. I'm not sure I'm ready for that. Anyway, this is Bramble, and Bramble this is Skinny Ali" I instinctively knew that the lad desperately wanted to say something, but the words seemed to be stuck, somewhere just below his knees. So he chose instead to nod and offer a flimsy wave to no one in particular.

Walking to the deli he finally found his voice. "Why Ali and Ali, I don't get it?"

"Because they're both called Alison of course," as if the answer was obvious. I'm pretty sure that this wasn't the first twenty minutes, in his very first fulltime, albeit temporary, job, that the lad had anticipated.

Next stop the deli to meet Elaine and Helen, and then back on to the morning jobs. But introductions were put on hold as Helen was getting something or other from out in the stockroom. Behind the counter Elaine stood ready for action, gesturing to us that we would have to wait, as she was just about to serve a customer, a lady, who if I was to guess wasn't much older than me. So from Bramble's perspective, clearly getting on a bit.

"I'd like to buy two olives please. One green and one whatever that colour is," pointing to the display of dark Kalamata olives.

With her smile tinged by a look of curiosity, Elaine answered. "I'm not sure I can sell you just two olives madam, because the scales wouldn't pick up any weight. In fact, the pot would probably be heavier than the olives. Can I ask why you are buying just two olives?"

"I've never had olives before, and I wanted to try them."

"Well, that's not a problem because I'm happy to let you try a couple for free." Offering the lady, first a green olive, in a plastic spoon, followed by the darker one.

Tasting each one in turn in what I thought to be a show of overly dramatic chewing. "Oh, they're nice aren't they. But I think I prefer the green one."

"Okay, so would you like a small pot of the green ones?" Which the lady agreed to. Delicately placing a generous quantity of green olives in the little plastic pot, Elaine then weighed them and stuck the resulting price ticket all the way over the pot to seal it securely. There was no way that lid was going to come off anytime soon. Offering the pot over. "You just need to take that to the checkout – enjoy your olives!"

However, the lady didn't take the pot as expected, she instead asked. "Can you put two of the darker olives into the pot as well please?"

Only someone that has been with a person for over thirty years, as I have with Elaine, would know when the tether has been well and truly stretched. Thankfully the customer remained oblivious, as Elaine continued to refuse the proffered pot of olives. "I'll tell you what I'll do madam, I'll put two of the Kalamata olives into a separate pot and you can have them, for free, how does that sound?"

"So, I'll have two pots then. And do I still need to take this other pot to the checkout as well?"

"That's right madam you'll have two pots, and no you won't need to take the other pot, the one with the two olives in, to the checkout, that'll be our little secret. Is there anything else I can help you with today?"

A great performance from a true professional deserving recognition. "That was really well done my dear."

"Mike what do you want!" Ah there you are.

"Nothing much I was just bringing Bramble over to introduce him to you, that's all. Bramble this is my wife, Elaine."

"Bramble, you say. Nice name, do you have any siblings?"

"Thanks, but I don't really like my name much. My dad named me after a footballer, Titus Bramble. And yeah, I have a brother called Barnaby."

"I think it's a great name. Look on the bright side you could have been called Titus. Imagine what the kids at school could have done with that." I could tell that he had instantly warmed to Elaine.

As we turned and walked away, he gave her a shy wave, and then turned to me. "Your wife is nice."

"Yeah, she is. Come on tell me about what you really want to do with yourself, as I'm guessing working in retail isn't it." And as we litter picked around the outside of the shop, he opened up to tell me how he hoped to become a top chef. Hence why he was going to college in September.

Do you work here? – The shop floor chronicles

Most unusual item found during my time litter picking around the perimeter of The Country Produce Store: A large pair of track suit bottoms. The most disgusting: A very used, unfolded disposable nappy. Most commonplace: Neatly tied off part filled dog poo bags. Most unusual item found in the car park by my wife: A child's car seat, without child.

Michael Ethelson

TEN

THE COUNTRY PRODUCE STORE WAS GETTING A
GREAT REPUTATION FOR OFFERING FOOD FOR THE
SOUL. MICHAEL OFFERS SOME FOOD FOR THOUGHT.

"Why is it that customers can't put their trolleys back where they need to be? I had a bloke bending my ear because a rogue trolley, left goodness knows where, had been blown by the wind and into the side of his car. Of course, it wasn't my fault but there was no telling him of course." This was Denise who on this particular occasion wasn't chuckling, she was near to tears.

During multiple lunchbreaks my colleagues often shared their frustrations – me included. Those things that couldn't be spoke of anywhere else, other than amongst ourselves, and in the relative safety of the staff restroom. Even members of the management team were known to let off a bit of steam from time to time. And the common topic of our conversations, grievances and annoyances would have been the conduct of some of our customers. And no, these weren't moans for moaning's sake or the comical / not so comical antics that you've been reading about, they were proper frustrations. Some of which have been listed below.

- Leaving a shopping trolley anywhere other than in the designated place.

- Spill or drop something on the shop floor and then ignore it.

- Take something off a shelf, walkaround a bit, decide that you don't want it and then dump it in some random spot. Especially irritating when the item in question happens to be cold or frozen goods.

- Ask for your receipt at the checkout and then throw it on the floor outside the shop.

- Date checking items by pulling them from the back of the shelf and then either leaving them in a random space or returning them to the shelf in a hap-hazard way. Or not putting them back on the shelf at all.

- Come into the shop at closing time and get annoyed when you're told that the place is closing. Remember – "But I need to buy a few things for our supper."

- Come into the shop a few minutes before closing and slowly saunter around as though you've been granted some kind of special perusing license.

- Name dropping the owners or managers names in the hope that you'll get preferential treatment. In my experience it never works by the way.

- Tutting, sighing, and staring at the till operator when there's a long queue at the checkout. Just so you know, making these noises won't make the queue move any quicker.

- Letting your small children run around the shop unsupervised. It really isn't cute when your child puts their finger through a bag of flour and shows you their little white pinkie.

- Decide you don't want something and then hand it to the checkout operator. Once again especially irritating when the item in question happens to be cold or frozen.

- Having a telephone conversation whilst you're being served.

- Being verbally or physically abusive to a shop floor person for any reason whatsoever.

- Pushing past or losing your patience with a shop floor person when they're clearly just doing their job.

- Giving the shop floor person a hard time if the carpark is full, if there's a car alarm going off, or there are no more disabled or mum and toddler car parking spaces available.

- Banging on the door at ten minutes before opening, just because you spotted someone on the shop floor.

Do you work here? – The shop floor chronicles

- When you take a paper bag for your loose fruit and vegetables, another one drops on the floor, and you just leave it there.

- Anything out of stock isn't the shop floor person's fault. There is really no point in giving them a hard time.

And finally -

- We know it's only a little puppy dog, but unless it is classified as an 'Assistance dog' then it cannot come into the shop. Raising your voice in protest at the shop floor person won't change your dog's classification.

Did you see any of yourself in that list?

ELEVEN

INVASION OF THE COFFEE MORNING MUMS. AND
MICHAEL STARTLES THE LAD WITH A COLLECTIVE
NOUN.

"Look we're the only ones in here. If you move that table next to this one and I move this table next to that one, and bring the one from over there to here, we can all sit together, but still have a table each. How splendid!"

Ladies and gentlemen, the coffee morning mums are in the building. And will be for at least the next two hours as they negotiate the challenge of consuming a single coffee.

It wasn't only the antics of the baby boomer entitled types that raised eyebrows and hackles amongst my shop floor colleagues, there were various others too. Particularly on school days when the coffee morning mums would often pay us a visit. These are a species of younger entitled types, although very much in a league of their own.

Having dropped their school age children off at school, these mums, with apparently little else to do, would come into the coffee shop with their preschool children and meet up with other coffee morning mums. Within minutes one became two and then three, but rarely more than four for some reason. Having rearranged the furniture to suit their needs, they would set about occupying a sizable area of the coffee shop with what appeared to be the contents of John Lewis's Baby & Child department. They then order their flat white oat milk decaffeinated something or other, which will subsequently take them about two hours to consume. One or two might go mad and dare to order a blueberry or chocolate muffin, and in doing so make it sound like they're committing the crime of the century. "Oh, I know I shouldn't but…." and then turning to their partner in crime. "What do you think? Do you think I should? Oh, this is all too much! Yes hang it all, I'm going to do it…." And then realising that there's an actual person behind the counter her demeanour changes in an instant. "Is that blueberry muffin gluten free?"

Here to help - *Gluten is Latin and means 'glue' and glutinous means 'glue like'. It's the gluten in flour which makes bread dough stretchy and gooey, or glutinous.*

"No madam, but I think you'll find that they're all very glutinous." Ah! The bewildered look on the face of the coffee morning mum was a sight to behold.

"What about fructose, is there any of that in there?"

"Probably in the blueberries madam."

"In that case I'll take one."

Just in case, like the average coffee morning mum, you're not sure - *Fructose is a sugar found naturally in fruits, fruit juices, some vegetables and honey.*

Two weeks in and Bram, as he prefers to be called, was becoming increasingly confident, but still struggled somewhat with things that people of my age seem to take for granted. Such as putting words together in a particular order so they make actual sentences, that you can then use to converse with. For instance talking on the telephone with another person, as opposed to holding a conversation solely through the medium of messaging. Likewise, getting him to see the benefits of using a pencil and paper to take notes, and not the notes app on the mobile phone, which he wasn't allowed to take onto the shop floor. Although he was getting better, and I enjoyed his company. So, as his self-appointed, albeit irregular, mentor, I thought it was time to raise the bar on his continued education.

Just outside the coffee shop door, and from the relative safety of the artisan cooking sauces, we were doing some replenishment. Whilst at the same time watching the rigmarole inside unfold. "Hey Bram, do you know what a collective noun is?" I ask.

"Is it a bunch of something, like grapes or bananas?"

"Yes, it is like a bunch of something as you say. But there are quite a few others, such a murder of crows, a gaggle of geese, a pack of mules or a particular favourite of mine, a nest of rumours." The look on his face strongly suggested that I needed to bring the bar down again. The lights were still on, but the curtains were now drawn. "Look what I'm driving at, is what collective noun do you think we could give to the coffee morning mums? As in all of them together, like a collection."

In an instant the curtains flew back, as he excitedly, almost conspiratorially, for fear of being overheard, announced. "I know, what about a collection of coffee morning mums!"

Ignoring the fact that I had just said the self-same words, and not giving in to the temptation to pour honey mustard dipping sauce onto his head, I ploughed on. "I was thinking of something a bit more 'out there' to be honest Bram." So, assuming that he was unlikely to be a valuable contributor to this endeavour, I continued to pass him jars and bottles to fill the gaps on the shelves. In the meantime, I whiled away the time by thinking of a suitable collective noun for this very unique species of customer. I thought of a drove, then not, because that's normally used for donkeys, or maybe a pandemonium, as in a pandemonium of parrots. But none of what I came up with seemed to capture the essence of what I saw in the characters taking up residence within the coffee shop. I needed to go off road.

"I know, I've got it – A Thicket! A Thicket of coffee morning mums!" It had been quite a few years since I'd made a twelve-year-old jump. The last time I did, if my memory serves me right, it was our son. I recall that he was quietly enjoying a poo when my foot came through the bathroom ceiling. I happened to be in the loft at the time looking for something or other and had inadvertently come to the end of the floorboarding. He subsequently leaped from his porcelain throne, and with trousers still around his ankles, tripped and banged his head on the washbasin. In his own way Bram was no less startled as I made 'The Thicket' announcement and was clearly unsure how to react, being confronted by this mad bloke holding aloft a jar of avocado ranch sauce, in a Eureka! kind of way.

But once he'd pulled himself together, he was on it. "What you mean as in thick, as in not very clever, kind of oblivious to the rest of the world. Yeah, I reckon you're on to something there, Mike!"

For the avoidance of any doubt relating to the use of the word 'thick' in this anecdote. *It is British slang where a thick person is considered to be slow-witted. Not, and I repeat, not, 'thick' as in hip hop slang from the early noughties. Where it supposedly means a sexually attractive woman, usually voluptuous or curvaceous.*

Our new collective noun was agreed upon and stock replenishment had never been so much fun.

Whilst The Thicket – yeah, I like it – with stupidity and oblivion coursing through their designer genes, are settling in, their preschool brood are now getting restless, crawling, and running riot in the coffee shop. Sachets of sugar, napkins, in fact anything at table height or lower is fair game for these spoiled monsters. But to give The Thicket their due they are ruthless in their discipline. "Oh, Jordy would you mind stopping that please, mummy's trying to talk." Or the severest of tongue lashings. "How about you come and sit here with mummy. You can have some of my muffin or how about mummy buys you your own babyccino?"

This was the first time I had heard of something called a babyccino and looked to Bram for enlightenment, but nothing was forthcoming other than a shrug. So, I looked it up on the phone that I wasn't supposed to have on the shop floor. *Babyccino – A coffee free cappuccino for the children. It was described as being a warm frothy milk drink to which marshmallows or chocolate powder can be added*. So, there it was. A sugar fix for a child that was already showing all the symptoms of being on liquid cocaine – perfect!

The resulting effect of this most rigorous of reprimands and numerous offers of inducement, being absolutely zilch. The mayhem continues, The Thicket are oblivious, and both Ali's are seething.

It's only with the arrival of the next wave of customers, mostly older sorts who have no problem with filling a space already taken, that cause The Thicket to disperse and move on and out into the shop. Now this is a much bigger playground for the pre-schoolers. Once they're loose in the shop the spree of vandalism increases exponentially, and no amount of chastising does anything to curb their enthusiasm. "Mummy's getting cross now!" says one of them, although to give her some due she does follow it up with decisive action. She reaches out to the confectionary display and places a bar of artisan chocolate into the child's tiny fist. The child in question stops immediately and climbs into its off-road capable stroller, clearly satisfied with a job well done. The other mummies are equally as implacable in their discipline. Some try to win them over with offers of biscuits or the promise of a trip to the play park. Whilst one really goes for it. "There's a good boy," to which the toddler agrees. Can this really be 21st century child rearing? I read somewhere that the growth in the UK's population is slowing. Not quick enough for the coffee shop Ali's though.

Calm is restored to The Country Produce Store and the carpark less full as four large German and British 4x4 SUV's leave, no doubt to reap chaos elsewhere. We know they'll be back, but for now let's just enjoy the peace and quiet, as we walk around the shop picking up all manner of produce from off the floor. Back in the coffee shop the two Ali's are looking like they need a stiff drink, with one of them gamely giving me a thumbs up followed by a great mime of hanging herself with an imaginary necktie from one of the Victorian oak beams. But then they're quickly called back into action as they have to deal with an elderly, clearly of the 'Entitled' variety, lady who is getting quite animated about the fact, that as a regular customer she doesn't understand why she's unable to get a table of her own in the coffee shop. The first come first served argument, calmly delivered by Ginger Ali, cuts no ice with this person of privilege as she demands to speak with a manager.

Quick question: When and how do these people become this way? Is it a gradual process or do they wake up one morning and decide; "That's it I'm just not going to bother to be civil anymore?" Or have they always been like it? That was three questions – sorry.

* * *

"How much is it to put an ad on your noticeboard? I've got a few things to sell you see. Some of my nan's old stuff." Announced a youngish lady holding what looked like half of one side of a breakfast cereal box with some writing on it, clearly done with a felt tip pen – or three. For some reason the letters in each of the words were a different colour.

Not having the inclination to question her dubious quixotry attempt at being artistic. "Fifty pence a month madam. Can I read through the list please." Apart from the size of the piece of card and the childish writing, there was nothing untoward with any of the objects for sale. Although I did think that the VHS video recorder and Orange shag pile rug (with some faded puppy wee stains) might be hard sells. But the thing that caught my eye was the 998-piece jigsaw – Austrian alpine scene. Looking up from the list, I enquired. "This item, the nine hundred- and ninety-eight-piece jigsaw. Seems like an odd number to me. I would have expected a round number like say, a thousand."

"Yeah, there are two pieces missing, which I reckon are down the side of the velvet three-seater sofa. The one for sale at the bottom of the list."

TWELVE

AWAY FROM THE MADDENING CROWD, IN
RECOUNTING THE DAPPER CHAP, THE NAUGHTY OLD
GIRL, AND THE HUMBLE CELEBRITY.

"The Martians have landed!"

Despite the few obtuse and belligerent customers determined to spoil my day there were many others who just made coming to work at The Country Produce Store so worthwhile.

Here we have an older gent, a frequent shopper, who always dressed dapperly. With impeccable manners and a sunny disposition. Whilst he's checking out one day – I mean from the shop not for good – he was to hold up a cucumber and start to recite an old Ken Dodd joke to me. One that I had already heard quite a few times over the years. In fact, and probably because I'm no spring chicken, I actually remember Ken Dodd telling this joke on TV a long while back. However, being the well-mannered fellow that I am, I let this dapper old gent continue to tell his joke and reacted to the punch line as if it were my first time. We both bellowed with laughter.

For those of you that don't know, *(Sir) Ken Dodd OBE - (1927 – 2018) was an English (music hall style) comedian, singer, and sometimes actor. Primarily known for his live stand-up performances that included a rapid and relentless delivery of often surreal jokes.*

The joke in question goes something like this – *What a wonderful day it is for pushing a cucumber through the mothers-in-laws letterbox and shouting, "The Martians have landed!"*

I never said it was a classic.

Over the months, as we moved from summer to autumn and as salad ingredients became less popular, he would present me with a courgette and recite the same joke. Then over time he progressed to just quoting the punchline. Approaching the checkout, and much to the surprise of people in the queue, he would hold up his cucumber (or courgette) and point it in my general direction. "The Martians have landed!" He would enthusiastically announce to the shop. We would both laugh in a kind of conspiratorial way, much to the quizzical looks of everyone else. Of course, we would never let them in on what was now *our* joke.

* * *

Taking being naughty to another level was a particular old lady, who I used to really look forward in seeing. A game old bird of probably eighty plus years if she was a day, with the wit of a music hall comic. I recall our first meeting. "You're new here, aren't you?"

"Yes I am. New to the shop although not to life." But I was to be completely disarmed, bound, and gagged within just a few seconds.

"Are you trying to chat me up?"

"No madam, nothing could be further from my mind." Which I can assure you was an absolute truth.

With a wry smile she was on it in a flash. "Why? Don't you fancy me then?"

Abort! Abort!

This lovely lady had an innuendo and riposte for everything I said, and so much more besides. But not blue rude, just naughty.

I remember on one occasion making the rookie error of asking her if she was okay with doing her own packing. I'll leave it to your imagination how that was responded to but suffice to say her voluble reply went something along the lines of. "What I choose to do in the privacy of my own bedroom is very much my own business, thank you very much young man." With each wrinkle on her face serving to enhance the huge smile as she spoke. While I in turn blushed like a spotty youth, not daring to look up at the wider audience – the checkout queue and the few of my colleagues who had chanced upon this impromptu encounter. The smarter I thought my comments the better her return. It was as though she had an inexhaustible repertoire. I was very much the straight man – or helpless observer – in this one-sided comedy act. And it was brilliant!

However, if the queue behind her started to get too long I'd reluctantly have to close the game down. If not, then it could often go on until she had me cornered into what a casual bystander might easily believe to be some dangerous, and oddly weird liaison. At some point – of her choosing – she'd let me off the hook by telling me that I was too old, too young, not wealthy enough… for her tastes. These harmless exchanges went on each time she was in the shop, and I happened to be on the checkout, much to the amusement of everyone else. I was no match for this lovely lady and gave up trying to compete. I concluded that sometimes in life it's just best to accept defeat when it's offered to you on a plate. Even if your adversary is eighty plus years of age. On occasion, if I happened to be out back in the stockroom it wouldn't be unusual to receive a message on my radio. "Mike to the checkout please, Mike to the checkout. Your girlfriend is in."

* * *

Finally, for now at least, there was this one gent, and arguably the favourite of all my customers. He was probably about fifteen or twenty years older than me, and neither funny nor difficult. One of those regular shoppers if you like. So why does he get a special mention? I'll tell you why. Because it was during one of those 'passing the time of day' type of chats whereupon he enquired about my life before The Country Produce Store. I then played a similar question back to him, regarding his life before he became a regular customer of ours. Almost embarrassingly, he revealed that he'd spent much of his life as a keyboard player for one of the most famous performers in the world. And no, I'm not going to tell you who. It was the way in which he, almost apologetically, dropped it into our conversation that really grabbed me. But even more than that, he was equally (and genuinely) enthralled by my career choice, asking me all manner of questions about my previous professional life, the companies I had worked for, the places I had been and so on. Here was one of life's gentle and genuine people who was interesting, worldly, subtly humorous but above all humble. Someone who just wanted to talk about anything other than his own interesting self. I would gladly pack his shopping bag at the checkout, where after much prompting on my part he'd regale me with quips of the music business he had given most of his life to. Of being on tour, the technologies of the recording studio, that he admitted he never really understood. But in doing so, never once in a sensational way and nor did he betray any confidence. In fact, in all the conversations we had, he only ever mentioned the artist he'd keyboarded for once. But the real story, which isn't his time as a keyboard player, or session musician for countless others, was that this unassuming fellow had been a solo artist in his own right. In the 1960's he'd had numerous hit records, selling millions, and with a couple of gold discs to boot.

I remember him telling me how he envied someone like me who clearly had no fear of technology and had chosen to come and work in a shop. Something he said he would never have the courage to do. He was very much a creature of habit, so it is with genuine regret that only a few of his designated shopping days coincided with my shift days. I let him know during one of our chats that Elaine, on the deli, was my wife. He was to go on and have similar chats with her. Some months later I casually dropped the subject of this lovely man into a conversation with others on the shop floor, being careful not to reveal anything I'd been told. I was to conclude by their casual responses that we (Elaine and I) were part of an exclusive club. He was of course known to them, but considered no more than just a regular customer, and that because he'd been seen in the store quite a few times. Such was his understated manner, some actually struggled to recall who I was talking about while others just shrugged as though he was no big deal. To them he was just a regular bloke, a shopper, which I reckon is exactly the way he liked it. As such I was honoured – and still am – to have been his conversation buddy. For a short while at least.

A few months after I'd left The Country Produce store, I was to discover that both Fran and Maureen also knew the back story to this lovely man. But they, like us, never felt the need to make a big deal about the fact.

Celebrity or naughtiness put to one side for a moment, what each of these fine people had in common was that they made me smile. So yes, I *did* have some great customers, great interactions, and do have many fond memories.

* * *

I was often left with a feeling of disappointment that more people couldn't be more like our dapper gent, the naughty lady or humble celebrity. However, despite what you have read prior to these fine examples of human beings, most days in The Country Produce Store went off without major incident. Neither entertaining nor irritating. In fact, quite monotonous if I'm being honest. That said I cannot recall a single day when there wasn't at least one episode or one person to talk about over dinner. Admittedly not all of them as entertaining as our dapper gent or as infuriating as the coffee morning mums, Spanish plum lady or the various troublemakers that seemed to cross our threshold. Though sadly there were many people, arguably too many, that just seemed to lack social grace or good manners. And yes, on occasion it did irritate me – a lot. Principally because I didn't understand why people felt the need to behave as they did.

Over time I was to learn a lot about human nature and how it manifests itself in certain behaviours, particularly in the retail environment. I also learnt a lot about myself. Unwittingly I cultivated another smile that says, "I absolutely agree with you." My wife says patronising. Those people who are most vociferous about their own rights often overlook the fact that other people, those of us on the shop floor for example, have rights too.

In recognition of this foreign state, I increasingly found myself adopting a position of actively demonstrating that certain behaviours just weren't acceptable. Although not in any direct or rude way, otherwise I'd be no better than the perpetrators.

Consider it as providing a public service if you like or even offering up some much-needed rehabilitation to those in need.

And I wasn't the only one thinking along these lines I can assure you. Older hands had developed similar mechanisms. In doing so giving themselves at least a fighting chance of coming out the other side of each day on the right side of normal. Although in an arguably less direct way than I had chosen to adopt. Each and possibly every day I was left wondering at how, as a society, so many people find it so easy to be so rude for no good reason. Whatever happened to good old-fashioned manners?

So, for the remainder of my time at The Country Produce Store the kid gloves stayed in my locker.

Having said all that, and as you have already read, not all the customers were arses. The majority of those that I interacted with were just your regular shoppers. People that simply came in and did what they needed to do without fuss or performance. Most being genuinely good, polite, humble human beings. Often keen to stop and have a chat, for which I was happy to oblige. No agenda, just some good old-fashioned chit-chat, about the weather or the amount of traffic on the road on whatever day they had chosen to venture out. As if cold weather in the winter and warm weather in the summer were somehow an unexpected occurrence that we needed to get to the bottom of.

It was these types of customers, plus our dapper chap, and all the others that made me laugh, smile, or held my interest for some reason or other, that made the job worthwhile.

However,…

THIRTEEN

BUSINESS AS USUAL COMES IN THE FORM OF A
COUPLE OF RANDOM, ALL TOO COMMON, ERRANT
BEHAVIOURS.

"Excuse me, you there, I want the rye bread that comes in a cellophane packet and has German writing on it!" Delivered by a quivering yet authoritative voice.

Not that customer behaviours were particularly seasonal, but I did find that as we moved from summer to autumn and the weather began to chill then so did their manners – even more so.

For this lady there was no apparent need for eye contact or a, "I would like," or "Please can I have," or even a "Good morning," just an instant demand. All from about 10 yards from where I was standing.

Exactly the sort of person I was referring to a few pages ago. Stepping closer to her and adjusting my smile accordingly. "Good morning, madam how are you today? So, let me get this right you would like rye bread, that is wrapped in a packet that you say has German writing on it – please?"

"Yes, that's what I said and I'm in a hurry!"

I now had two choices. Either tell her that we do not sell rye bread or something else. Trust me I was tempted with the 'something else' option but I chose instead for the former. "Ah okay madam, but sadly we don't actually sell rye bread. Tell me are you sure that you bought the rye bread you're looking for, here?"

"It was either here or the local supermarket, I can't be expected to remember everything, can I now!" Berating me as if it were my fault that her memory was failing almost as much as her manners.

"Of course not madam, I apologise, but I can assure you that it wouldn't have been here because as I say we don't sell rye bread."

"No that can't be right. Can I suggest that you ask someone in authority because I'm pretty sure you're new here, am I right?"

"Yes, you're right madam. By comparison to some of my colleagues I am indeed relatively new here. However, that aside, there would still be no point in asking someone in authority because as I say I do know, for sure, that we do not sell rye bread, of any denomination.

"Just try won't you!"

"Yes of course, madam, I will always endeavour to do just as you suggest." Enough was enough. Some things I'll put up with, but I draw the line at being barked at. Meaning that it was about time that choice two – something else – was brought into play. Putting on the 'I absolutely agree with you,' smile that I was telling you about earlier, I continued. "Of course, madam, and to make sure I get my story straight when I go to speak with the whole management team, tell me does the wrapper have to have German writing on it? For example [pause for dramatic effect] in the unlikely event that we do happen to have a stray loaf of rye bread out in the stockroom, and it came in a wrapper with say English or even Danish writing on it, would that do?"

"I don't know, but I remember that the rye bread is black."

I was so tempted to ask if she would consider other colours, but I didn't. So decided instead to tell her that I would just pop out back and make some enquiries for her. "If, in the meantime, you would like to peruse the bakery shelves for some bread that we actually do sell, then feel free. I'll just be a few ticks."

After a few gulps of my morning cuppa, a quick check in with Fran at Goods In, I came back on to the shop floor and delivered the bad, but not new, news that we do not do rye bread of any type. At which point, and I guess predictably, she didn't give me a thank you for trying, or further acknowledgement of my being there, she simply turned and walked away. I in turn gave her the best cheery farewell that I could muster. "Bye bye then, thanks for popping in!"

And yes, I know I was wrong on so many of the 'delivering happiness to customers' levels but sometimes the devil needs a day out too. Nothing more to say.

* * *

Surgical mask wearing in public places such as shops has remained commonplace in the aftermath of the COVID pandemic. And although such behaviours are now more relaxed there are still many places and people preferring to continue with such precautions. Something I regard as a personal choice and therefore have no view on. Until recently my dentist still insisted that I wear a mask whilst in the waiting room, whereas my doctor's surgery doesn't. Maybe it's because my dentist considers my face to be particularly offensive and therefore insisting I wear a mask as a necessary precaution against me scaring other patients. As for my doctor he's probably seen a lot worse so is more relaxed about my male equivalent of a 'resting bitch face'. The couple I'm about to tell you about are avid mask wearers or more accurately, avid 'nearly' mask wearers. You will understand more about what I mean by that as we go through the story.

An elderly couple, who I'd seen in the shop on quite a few occasions, are as I say avid surgical mask wearers. A harmless pair who over the years it would seem have grown into becoming almost a single being. The level at which they both stoop is perfectly matched, so neither have to raise their head in order to look across at the other. I have heard them ask and answer a question to one another in a single perfectly timed breath, as well as walking and turning corners in perfect unison. As I say they are quite harmless, until that is one or other needs the toilet. Which was the case on this particular day. I wasn't to know what their specific need was, as I was head down and determined to finish the job I'd been given, so I might treat myself to a lunch break. There was a meat pie waiting for me, with literally my name on the bag, that I had asked Elaine to set aside for me. Looking up I saw them both, as one, heading in my direction. Not at speed mind you but more of an amble really. Almost as if they were hovering a few inches above the floor and being taken along by the gentle breeze that tends to flow through the shop, when the entrance and exit doors are both open. So, I had plenty of time to hatch an escape plan. To be honest the speed at which they were travelling I reckon there would have been enough time to have dug an actual escape tunnel out and into the carpark, complete with a complex array of wooden support braces. As it was, I opted for a simpler means by which to avoid their attention and decided upon a quick sidestep, to hide behind the locally produced – in Italy – dry pasta display. However, Sharon, who was busy having an altercation with a half-wit, was unaware of the encroaching couple.

Replenishing newly delivered milk into the cold cabinet, a middle-aged bloke decided to empty ALL the crème fraiche and double cream pots into his trolley. Stepping aside, Sharon then watched as he sorted through the whole lot, clearly looking for the best 'use by' dates. Having selected a single pot of each he then unloaded his trolley, putting the remaining produce back into the cold cabinet. All good so far and no need for Sharon to accost him –

yet. Until that is he mixed the crème fraiche and double cream together on the same shelf, with some of the pots being placed upside down. To cap it all, either because he was in a hurry, an idiot or not competent in the art of putting things on a shelf (or all three), he had a surplus. Which, for some inexplicable reason he made the mistake of trying to hand to Sharon. "What is it that you think you're doing sir!"

"I wanted to make sure that I got the best 'use by' date."

"Yeah, I see that but I'm not sure it was absolutely necessary to empty the whole display. And I'm guessing that putting things back as you found them was out of the question, right?" Complete with a gaze that could boil milk.

Clearly lacking intelligence and not being qualified to out stare Sharon, he simply made a weak apology and walked away. Leaving her to fume. But with the recovery rate of a seasoned warrior, and as water runs off a grizzly bears head, she came down quickly and the half-wit was already a distant memory.

At seeing my disappearing act the elderly couple simply turned and headed towards an unsuspecting Sharon. Their slick turning put me in mind of when I was a kid and particularly sports day. I remember participating in something called the three-legged race. Once an extremely popular sports day event in primary schools, but not so much these days by all accounts. In fact, I read somewhere that it's actually been banned in some schools, citing health and safety concerns. According to one report, *the ban was due to a likelihood of children falling over*. Imagine that, children falling over, whatever next. Anyway, if you don't know, the race entailed two children standing side by side and having their adjacent legs tied together with a scarf or skipping rope. Against other conjoined pairs, they'd be expected to do a 100-yard dash down the running track. Few pairs finished the race and those that did cross the finishing line had figured out that the best approach wasn't to run at all, but to walk – albeit faster than your competitors. Much like our elderly couple, although in their case taking the three-legged race to a whole new cautious level. The way they turned was indeed as though their adjacent legs were somehow tied together. Maybe as a couple of childhood sweethearts they'd competed in the race together and decided against removing the scarf or skipping rope?

It wasn't until a shadow crept across the cold cabinet that Sharon became aware of the old couple, as they lent in and then one (or both) of them asked. "Is there a toilet nearby?"

Still feeling a tiny bit tetchy I'm guessing. "If you're going to wear a surgical mask shouldn't it be over your mouth as well as your nose?"

"But then we can't breathe properly, and we wouldn't be able to understand one another, is there a toilet nearby?" A perfect acapella duet.

Stepping slightly away. "Yes there is, towards the back of the coffee shop."

"What all the way back over there?" The couple now adopted the look of a pair of owls looking back over their shoulders but keeping their feet facing Sharon.

All the way back over there was about 100 feet – slightly less than 30 metres for the benefit of younger readers and non-golf players.

"Yes!" says Sharon.

"Don't you have a toilet that's a bit closer?"

"No, we don't." Sharon was always economic with words. Unless she was berating me that is.

"Well maybe you ought to." And with that they simply turned on an invisible turntable and walked away to navigate the 100-foot journey to the coffee shop. But in doing so they would now be going against the prevailing breeze. So not only having to deal with the need for a toilet, but also the prospect of an even slower journey back up the shop. I hoped their call of nature wasn't an urgent one.

"It's alright you can come out now Mike," said Sharon as she quickly finished up the replen job and made her way to the safety of the stockroom.

Michael Ethelson

FOURTEEN

IN WHICH A LADY FARTS AT THE CHECKOUT AND
MICHAEL IS CAUSED TO SERIOUSLY CONSIDER
WHETHER A FUTURE IN RETAIL WAS INDEED THE
RIGHT CAREER CHOICE.

"Can I put a little For Sale card on your noticeboard?"

LOVELY BUT OLDER KING CHARLES FOR SALE. VACCINATED AND MICROCHIPPED.

"That's perfect thank you. That'll be fifty pence for the month please."

Being on the checkout meant that we were often the first port of call for things such as this. People wanting to sell stuff via our noticeboard or to advertise a local business and all manner of forthcoming events. I had been working the tills, on and off since I started at the shop. And apart from the fruit and veg it was one of the first things I was shown. During that time, and up to the point where me and The Country Produce Store parted company, I had both the pleasure and pain of having to deal with a wide range of people, their behaviours, and all manner of situations. Some of which I will share as we go through this chapter.

Within The Country Produce Store, we had two and a half tills or checkout points. The half till was situated off the beaten track to one side of the other two. It could easily have been mistaken for a small clerk's booth. Or should I say a small booth for a normal sized clerk – you have to be so careful these days. It was generally only used as a dumping ground for items such as freebee magazines, carrier bags, spare till rolls and the like. And because it still sported its Perspex COVID protector screen it also acted as an overflow for the main customer noticeboard, which was generally given over to things for sale. This one however was the place where you would find a whole variety of local notices. Bingo at the village hall, gardening services – none of whom were lady gardeners, local artisans who were able to make things out of driftwood, and for some reason a disproportionate number of dog care ads. Walking, grooming, dog sitting (as in babysitting not teaching dogs to sit), puppy training and so on. However, there was one notice, now starting to show its age, which had been there long before my arrival, often attracting the wrong kind of attention. No one knew if the business in question was still operating, but it was left up purely for entertainment value, and I'm guessing the bit of eye candy. This being the picture of a burly country lad standing in a field, surrounded by cattle. The words at the bottom of the poster read:

LOCALLY REARED BEEF BOX AVAILABLE FOR CHRISTMAS. GRASS REARED, HIGH WELFARE, DRY AGED. Telephone Rob 24/7 on [phone number]

The only time that this booth wasn't used as a dumping ground or noticeboard would have been during public holiday weekends, Christmas, and Easter, when an increase in customer numbers demanded that it was called into action as a working checkout. An obsolete till machine would be brought from out back, dusted down and put into operation. However, with its operating system some decades behind the rest of the shop network, which was decades behind the rest of the modern world, it would often decide, mostly during our busiest periods, that enough was enough and just stop processing payments. Management was aware of the problem but would tell us. "As it's only used from time to time, we can't really justify buying a replacement."

Not unusually it would have been the shop floor team who were left having to defend and apologise for the malfunctioning, not fit for purpose equipment. I recall talking to someone who worked in a proper large supermarket about our dodgy substitute till. To which she told me that their tills are all modern so rarely broke down in the way that I described. However, it wouldn't be unusual for their IT department to make some remote upgrade, mostly overnight, resulting in the whole system having to be reset multiple times during the following day. Often at the busiest of times. And like us it would be their shop floor team that ended up having to face the flak from customers.

The good news on that front was that we didn't have an IT department to worry about. IT was dealt with remotely by a man called Derek who, according to Gavin, was there at the birth of retail technology during the 1980's. Having met Derek just the once I was left to ponder two things. The first being that the remote support that Gavin referred to was likely being provided from Derek's care home bed. And secondly, which would be likely to keel over first, our IT system or Derek. Although aged he was still full of bravado when we met, trying to baffle me with popular retail acronyms such as EPOS (Electronic Point of Sale), to which I offered an arguably more realistic alternative – Electronic Prehistoric Outdated System. Derek and I were never going to see eye to eye. To him I was a young fifty-eight-year-old IT upstart, and to me he was some silly old biffer that used to know something about computers. But to Gavin, Derek was cheap and therefore perfect for the job.

Back in The Country Produce Store we usually had two tills operating at any one time. And as an overhang from the COVID pandemic, when people were encouraged to pay by card only, only one of the two tills would normally take cash (and bank cards) whereas the other only accepting bank card payments, mobile phone, or wristwatch payments. I often wonder what my gran would make of that if she were alive.

Another COVID remnant, for some of the time I

was there, was the clear plastic barrier, installed to maintain necessary distancing or indeed any human contact whatsoever between us and the customers. Did that stop people from wandering into our space? Of course, it didn't. Although to be fair much of this encroachment was as a direct result of those that continued to where masks. Trying to have detailed conversations through a surgical or other homemade mask was often difficult. Some people genuinely struggled to hear what was being said, me included, whilst others were just plain deaf – again me included. Consequently after a few, "Pardons," and, "Can you repeat that please," many of our customers would just wander round behind the screen to get into hearing range. Sometimes just a few inches away.

Unlike many supermarket checkouts ours were a simpler affair. For example, there were no conveyor systems just a small platform where customers could place their shopping baskets or unload the contents of their trolleys. With the till set in the middle there was another small platform, just off to the till operators left, where, after their items had been scanned, they would be placed for bagging. Or as happened on many occasions, I would scan the goods and put them straight into the customers bag, as we passed the time of day chatting about the weather, their latest visit to the doctor, or some other trivia.

Given the choice I would opt to operate the 'card only' till. Shopping scanned, tap your payment card, get on with our lives, happy days. However, …

* * *

"This till is card only sir (or madam), is that alright for you?" Would be my usual opening line complete with my best welcoming smile. Though my wife insists that what I claim to be my best welcoming smile isn't very welcoming at all. Quite the opposite it would seem.

To which, if they were intending to pay by card or similar method as opposed to cash, then they would often say something along the lines of. "Yes that's fine thanks." And up they'd stroll.

One morning this was pretty much how it went down and exactly as I liked it. However, having scanned one particular gentleman's shopping there followed a pause. He then looks at me. "Can I get cashback on my card?"

"You could have done at the other till sir, but not at this one as it's for card payments only." Hoping that the request for cash was a slip of the tongue and realising his mistake he'd then bugger off. But he wasn't done yet.

"But I've had cashback before in this shop so what's changed?"

"Nothing's changed at all sir, it's just that this is a card only till, as such I have no cash to give you." I even opened the till drawer so that he could see that there was nothing inside, except copy till receipts and some paperclips.

"You said I can get cashback at the other till?"

I could see exactly where this was going. "Yes, sir you could have done. Had you checked out at that till then yes you would have been able to have gotten cash back. And there's a good reason for that, and that is because *that* till has cash in it." And yes, I know there were a lot of 'that's' in that dialogue. But that's how I talk when I get riled.

"But how was I to know that you don't have cash in your till?" He was, if not the sharpest pencil in the box, persistent.

Because it's a card only till you dimwit...!

Anyway, long story short and being a bloke rapidly getting to the end of his tether, I transferred the sale to my colleagues till, which as I've said did have cash in it, and got on with my life.

Although the bloke in question still wasn't finished with me yet. In taking his shopping to the other till he found it necessary to offer me some advice – I used to get that a lot from customers. "Don't you think that it would be a good idea if there was cash in your till as well, for the purposes of providing cash back?" I of course thanked him for his advice, whilst thinking how much of a meal he might make for our free-range pigs. I could have continued the dialogue I guess, by suggesting to him that if the 'card only' till had cash in it then it wouldn't be a 'card only' till anymore. Added to that the likelihood of having to bat away customers who wanted to do a cash transaction at said till, and not understanding why they couldn't when it clearly had cash in the drawer. Ranting inside my own head was becoming an increasingly common trait.

Instead, I just turned to serve the next customer. Who it turned out knew exactly what a 'card only' till was.

To customers who think they know best: Have you never wondered why there isn't a suggestion box in your local shop? And if a shop does happen to suggest that 'your opinion counts,' don't believe a word of it.

I remember asking management if we could have a sign put up on the 'cash only' checkout, clearly telling people that there was no cash in this particular till. Apparently, it was a great idea but up to the day I left the employ of The Country Produce Store no sign appeared – Hey Ho!

As the late great Terry Wogan used to say, – "Is it me?"

* * *

I guess in many ways The Country Produce Store, along with other farm type shops, garden centres etc that I've been to, the checkout arrangements are not dissimilar to that of the discount type supermarkets. But that's where the similarity ends. For example, in our local discount supermarket you load your goods onto the one side and quickly have to race to the other as your goods are scanned and moved into the smallest of receiving areas at hypersonic speed. Any ideas of orderly bagging on your part are well and truly scuppered, because rarely do you get to place more than one or two items into your shopping bag before… "Do you have a loyalty card and are you paying by cash or card today sir?" Your shopping is still in a pile, and you are being expected to pay and make way for the next person – pronto! No time for chit chat, just, 'take your discounted groceries and leave the premises immediately' type of system.

You're inevitably left with little choice other than to put everything back into the trolley or basket and move across to one of the handy bagging areas – or leave the shop altogether. These bagging areas are placed thoughtfully at the edge of the shop for use by the more discerning bag packer, or a place where you can just stop and draw breath. I've seen many of the uninitiated with a look of, 'what just happened to me!' as they wheel their trolley load of groceries out to the carpark, not even bothering to use the bagging area, no doubt to empty its contents straight into the boot of their car.

But the one thing I have noticed is how the queuing public are complicit in sponsoring this system, despite being treated in the same way come their time to check out. I saw one revolutionary determined that she wasn't going to be rushed, carefully placing her items into her shopping bag despite things continuing to pile up.

The shop floor worker on the till, who, let me add isn't responsible at all for this imposed method of checking out, is at a real loss what to do. Which I completely understand. However, it was the reaction of the queuing public that confounded me. They are no longer a queue of individuals, because in an instant they have become a pack. In the case of our rebellious bag packer, I was to witness them all, as a collective, moaning and groaning. Exchanging raised eyebrows to one another. Further embarrassing the shop floor worker on the till and putting undue pressure on the lady who wanted nothing more than to pack her shopping into a bag.

Within The Country Produce Store, it was nothing like that. I was encouraged to engage with the customers but not be overly attentive – which you might be surprised (or not) to hear I found quite easy to do. Gauge the type of customer, even assess their mood, adjusting my behaviours accordingly. Never be rude to customers and remember 'the customer is always right'. Well, you already know my thoughts on that. But how about an alternative tagline – which although wouldn't necessarily look good on a poster, is somewhat more aligned to my way of thinking; *'assume the customer to be an imbecile, until they prove themselves otherwise.'*

* * *

During quiet times I would, from my vantage point at the checkout, often watch the behaviours of many of the customers. Noticing for instance how we, the shop floor workers, are literally invisible as couples argue, share confidences, or have private conversations normally reserved for the bedroom. I've been told that it is often the same for people who work behind a bar. Where people lose sight of the fact that there is another human being just a few yards away, casually eavesdropping, as they argue or share their most intimate of secrets with one another – and the bar person.

If a couple were heavily engrossed in a topic of conversation that clearly couldn't wait until they got home, I would consciously take a step backward to afford them some privacy. If, however, their voices became raised I would make myself known by stepping out from behind my small counter as if something of importance had caught my attention in amongst the confectionery. Yep, even The Country Produce Store had a selection of chocolates and sweets displayed near the checkout. Albeit luxury after dinner mints or artisan chocolates. At which point any heated discussions would often instantly die away. If the topic of conversation happened to be of a particularly intimate nature the couple in question, having noticed a third person in their ménage – me – would likely approach the checkout in a sheepish fashion, pay for their shopping, being overly polite throughout the whole transaction, and leave without looking back. On other occasions if the conversation was a bit heated, bordering on a full-blown argument then it would not be unusual for it to continue at the checkout. Manifesting itself from being a verbal onslaught into a more demonstrative one. So not wanting me to be a witness to their obvious disagreement they would stop talking to one another altogether. One of them might even step away from the till leaving the other to deal with the groceries. Throughout the whole transaction prudence demanded that it would be best not to ask, how their day was going so far, as well as keeping my farewells to a bare minimum. So, anything such as, "Have a lovely evening," was off the menu. As for the couple who had inadvertently shared some bedroom gossip with me. "Have a lovely evening," seemed superfluous in a different way. Because they clearly already had plans in place to do just that.

Another thing about being on the checkout is that it often made me and my colleagues the focal point for a range of enquiries, and other attention. Some welcome, some not so. And I'm not referring to the occasional request for an Ad to be placed on our noticeboard. This type of attention wasn't dissimilar I guess to being that first point of contact for the crazies, when I was working the fruit and veg. Here though people were under some illusion that because I was on the till then I must possess a lot more general knowledge than someone who was engaged elsewhere in the shop. It wouldn't be unusual for a customer to walk through the shop, often passing any number of my colleagues, approach the checkout and ask something arbitrary. "Can you tell me what time you're open over the holidays?" was frequently asked – the shop opening, and close times were published at the entrance, exit, online and on various social media channels. Or else "Are you expecting a delivery of [such and such] anytime soon?" Or, as one woman once asked me. "Do you know what time the garage down the road closes?" But my favourite of all. "Do you think it would be okay to give this meat pie to my dog?"

* * *

Meandering up to the till with a basket of shopping came an elderly lady, decked out in tweed like clothes and sensible brown town shoes, who immediately demanded of me, in one of those well-honed authoritarian kinds of voices. "Well! Where do you want me?" Of course, there was no good afternoon, or where would you like me to place my basket of shopping. Not a chance from this most accomplished, fully paid-up member of The Entitled club.

Do you work here? – The shop floor chronicles

"How about six feet under madam?" Immediately checking myself and deciding instead to keep my thoughts inboard. And yes, I know it was harsh, but any grocery retail honeymoon that I may have had was well and truly over by the time this obstreperous woman came visiting.

"How about here madam – pointing to the right-hand platform – the very same spot that everyone else places their shopping as it happens?"

"But that means I have to walk all the way around there." All the way round there, incidentally, was about another three feet from where she was already standing.

"Yes, that's right madam, all the way round there." Continuing to smile of course.

Having arrived at our agreed destination she then proceeded to place her basket of shopping on the counter, handed me her shopping bag and turned around to engage in conversation with another baby boomer. In doing so, clearly expecting me to unload her shopping from the basket and pack it into the provided bag. With a small queue forming I decided to bury my pride and did exactly that. "Excuse me madam, sorry to interrupt, but that'll be ***forty-nine pounds and seventy-four pence,** please. How are you intending to pay today, card or cash?"

*The amount due has been highlighted for good reason – you'll see.

She then afforded me the honour of disengaging herself from whatever conversation she was having and handed me her payment card. "I'm sorry madam, but you will have to do this bit yourself. You'll notice that the card payment machine has been handily placed right in front of you."

Having placed her card in the machine – she could have probably got away with just tapping her card on the top, but I was in no mood to tell her – she then made an announcement to the shop. "I've forgotten my PIN!" Then looking straight up at me. "Do you know my PIN?"

Do you remember me telling you how wealth and age do not necessarily equal common-sense or intellect?

So, I said – and make no apologies for doing so. "Of course madam we keep a record of all of our customer's PIN's."

"Do you really?"

"No not really, I tell you what, remove your card from the machine and just tap it on the top, that should work." Which it did. "Would you like your receipt madam?"

"No, I wouldn't," brusqueness returning in an instant, and then continuing. "I'm unlikely to forget **forty-seven pounds and ninety-four pence** now, am I?"

"No madam, absolutely not, my apologies for even suggesting such a thing."

She then proceeded to turn tail and leave the shop all the while muttering something or other to her friend. None of which included a goodbye or thank you.

* * *

Some troublemakers bypassed the fruit and vegetables, the rest of my colleagues. and hightailed it straight to the checkouts.

A not so old fellow – what I mean by that is someone about the same age as me – decked out for the golf course in a pair of brightly coloured slacks and an ill-fitting pullover, purposefully strides up to the till. Under his arm is a locally baked large granary loaf which he then presents to me. "This loaf of bread is really expensive."

The first thing that struck me was the fellow hadn't even bothered to put the loaf into one of our bakery bags, with my eyes being drawn to the large patch of flour under his arm. No actually that's not true. The first thing that struck me was how ridiculous he looked in his flamboyant golf garb strutting around a farm shop. "Sorry that you think that sir. But as a small matter of interest may I ask what you're comparing its price to?" Trust me when I tell you that it really was a small matter of interest for me.

"Compared to the price of a granary loaf of bread in our local supermarket," he replied, together with a look of absolute self-satisfaction that was saying – Gotcha!

This wasn't the first time that I'd had to swat one of these accusations away. At around the same time it had been the locally brewed bottled craft ale that came under the spotlight.

Though to be honest as far as I was concerned, I wasn't employed to either justify or defend the prices that The Country Produce Store charged, so I guess I could have let it go, agreed with him even – after all 'the customer is always right', remember? Just let this fashion victim have his five minutes of whatever and I could then get on with my own life.

But there was something about this bloke, maybe it was the loaf under his arm or the 'Gotcha' look. "You may well be right sir, however the loaf in question was made fresh this morning by a local award-winning artisan baker, using only local produce. Which means that you won't be able to buy this actual loaf, nor indeed any of our bread, in any supermarket." Then giving him the best smile that I could muster at eight in the morning. "How would you like to pay this morning sir, card or cash?"

"Oh I don't want to buy it I just wanted to bring it to your attention that's all." And with that attempted to hand me the loaf.

Excuse my language and rest assured, and as tempting as it was, these words never left my mouth, but – "What the Fuck!"

I'm not a morning person so my hackles, which were already on high alert, were now well and truly raised. Although with my poker face firmly fixed you would never have guessed as much. There was no way I could let this go unchallenged. Keeping a straight face (my smile had slipped somewhat) and not making any move to accept the proffered loaf. "I'm sorry sir I don't understand. Regardless of your intentions you've not only handled the loaf, but you have carried it through the shop, under your arm and at no point has it been in a bag. I'm sure you understand that there's no way now that we can sell that loaf of bread to anyone else. Meaning that it will probably have to go to waste."

Maybe you will or maybe you won't believe what his reply was but here goes. "But how else was I going to bring it to your attention?"

I'm now on the verge of boiling and screaming inwardly to myself. "There was no need to bring it to my or anybody else's attention in the way that you did you moron!" And breathe…

"I guess if I was inclined to do such a thing, I'm not sure I would need the actual loaf as a prop." And breath once more… "You'll have to give me a moment as I need to call for assistance, as there are people behind you that look like they're actually going to buy some bread." You may have noticed how I'd lost my inclination to consider him as 'sir' by now.

With a queue forming and my inner self raging, back up was becoming increasingly necessary before I set about inserting said loaf into his ear. I therefore radioed for assistance to come to the till. In doing so I also requested for someone in authority to attend what could soon become a crime scene. Sharon came to operate the second till and Maureen emerged, or rather glided, from the back of the shop. I relayed the story to her, and in that moment, I saw her years of experience come to the fore. Without ceremony or fuss she simply smiled at the gentleman, and guided him by the elbow, complete with loaf, to a quiet corner of the shop. "Come this way sir I'm sure that we can work this out."

Foolishly he was heard to be trying to justify his

actions. "But I just wanted to make a point that's all and the fella on the till took it personally."

"Do you wish to buy the loaf sir?" I heard her say. I'd seen this approach before. At school when my headteacher, who like Maureen, never needed to raise his voice. He would calmly admonish you, almost in whispers, to the point where you not only admitted to the actual crime in hand, but also quite a few others besides – for good measure. In doing so offering a reassurance that you would never reoffend.

"Yes I understand that you wanted to make a point, but let me ask you again sir, do you wish to buy the loaf or not?"

"No, I was just …Never mind."

"In that case sir you have yourself a lovely day." Adding, should he have any doubts regarding his behaviour. "Perhaps next time we see you sir, and you should once again feel the need to prove a point, maybe you could do it in some other, less, obtuse way."

The next I saw of him he was leaving the shop in haste, head down, without the loaf and looking suitably admonished. Maureen then beckoned me to a quiet corner of the shop. Now it was my turn. "Michael, I know I only need to say this once. It's not your job to get into any type of altercation with any customer. Amongst other things that is what I get paid to do."

Suitably scolded and choosing not to offer any defence, I returned to the till. I thought it wise to keep shtum about the multiple other tête-à-têtes that I'd had since starting at the place. The same applied to any future ones. But on that day, I was extremely grateful for her intervention before the bonehead in question – I still haven't got over it – ended up in A&E having an artisan loaf surgically removed from some orifice or other. With me in turn ending up with a police record for GBH (Granary Bread Homicide) and losing my job as a result.

* * *

Even being on the checkout didn't afford me protection from the occasional fruitcake, who had the habit of turning up in various guises. But not all were unpleasant experiences, in fact some were an absolute delight.

One particular fellow, a regular cheese buyer, who liked a chat was one such character. I must have met this gent quite a few times and each time he would greet me as if it were our first. I'd often start the greeting with something that suggested that we had in fact met before. "Hello again, what cheese have you gone for today sir?"

As always, he would ignore my question, but not in any malicious way. "Good morning young man, how are you? You're new here, aren't you? Are you liking it?"

I was always 'young man' despite me telling him my name, on numerous occasions. "I'm well thank you and yes I like it here very much, thanks for asking." – again.

"I am partial to a bit of cheese you know." Of course I did know he was partial to a bit of cheese because he always told me so. After which we would move onto how I'd retired and now work here for a few days a week. At which point he would tell me that I looked too young to retire and what did I do before and so on. I'd of course tell him (again). Not quite a Groundhog Day moment every week but close. Now you might think that I'm poking fun at this cheese loving gent. And I guess yes, to a certain extent you would be right. But this gentle fellow just made me smile because more than anything he always seemed glad to see me, but more importantly I was always glad to see him – on each and every one of our first times. But still a fruitcake.

* * *

On another occasion there was this old girl who I'd never seen before. If I were to guess I would say that she must have been well into her seventies, possibly older. Extremely well turned out, though not in an ostentatious way but a smart Marks & Spencer kind of way.

She arrived at my till with a single jar of chutney lying in the bottom of a trolley. Nothing else just a jar of chutney. Upon arrival, and unloading her shopping, she felt it necessary to confide in me. "I've just had lunch in the village pub you know," adding, in a stage whispering conspiratorial way, "I think I may have had one too many white wines," followed by a chuckle and a little hiccup.

I instantly liked her. Though I was still baffled as to why there was only one item in her trolley. "Were you planning on doing more shopping today, but then had a change of mind madam?" Quickly following up with, "you're not driving are you madam?"

Having spent a few seconds contemplating what I

had said, she just looked up at me, smiled and proceeded to let go of a really impressive fart! At least a 'four seconder' by my calculations.

"Oops!" she announced to the shop, then quickly putting her hand to her mouth, as though, or perhaps hoping, that was where the noise had radiated from.

For a moment there was absolute silence and all eyes seemed to be on me. It was as though the whole shop was on tenterhooks waiting for me to move the situation on and into a safe place. The weight of expectation on my shoulders at that moment was immense I can tell you. An ideal time to have an epiphany of sorts. Come up with something gloriously profound, witty, memorable even. As it turned out none that happened. "Feeling better now madam, better out than in I always say. How would you like to pay today, card or cash?" To make matters worse, out of the corner of my eye, I noticed Sharon looking at me, mouth agape. Choosing to carry on as if nothing untoward had just happened I took the lady's money for her jar of chutney, watched her totter towards the door, abandon her trolley in a disabled carparking bay and climb into a waiting car. Thankfully she wasn't driving after all. I then turned to look at Sharon. "Are you okay?"

Still looking slightly incredulous she said, "I can't believe you called her out on that."

"As impressive as it was, I hope you're not suggesting that I should've taken the rap for that. Next customer please."

* * *

You may be surprised to hear that despite my best

efforts I only ever had one official complaint made against me. With the emphasis being on the word 'official.' Reason being, there was a bloke who felt it necessary to have a bit of a grumble to Maureen, because I refused to write a 'use by date' on a paper bag containing a single lettuce – she also refused as it happens. She instead chose to give him a particularly and unnecessarily lengthy tutorial on how to care for his lettuce once he had got it home.

Anyway, as far as my one and only 'official' complaint is concerned, I think now is as good a time as any to share that event with you.

"I've come to collect my order of six dozen eggs, four organic spelt loaves, two litres of organic semi skimmed milk, in one litre cartons, and three large pork pies." Said a lady with a surprisingly deep but unsurprisingly condescending voice. Someone who I'm guessing spends a lot of her time on a high horse – figuratively speaking – when it comes to dealing with people.

By now I had gotten used to certain people not bothering to meet and greet in a polite manner, so I got straight down to business. "No worries, madam, what's the name please?"

"Oh, surely you must know who I am!" adding, "I don't think I've had the pleasure, are you new here?"

Puts me in mind of a story my eldest daughter once told me, when she was working in a large department store. A well-known professional footballer had made a purchase, and my daughter needed his details to fill out the extended warranty.

"I'm sure you know who I am, so you don't mind if I don't give you my address do you?" In doing so finding it necessary to make some kind of comic book tittering sound. She did of course know who he was but wasn't in any mood to let on. Though she was impressed that a footballer had managed to put all those words together, and in the right order, to make a sentence – we're a rugby family. Shrugging and shaking her head in a display of ignorance, he was obliged to tell her his name. Adopting a nonplussed look. "I'm sorry but can you spell it for me sir?" That's my girl!

Back to my lady on her high horse. She of course hadn't yet had the pleasure of me, and I was pretty confident that she never will. "No madam I'm sorry I don't know who you are, but then I've only been here for just over seven months." All said with a pleasant, though condescending, smile on my face, with of course the usual hint of irony, reserved exclusively for these types of people.

"Seven months you say! In which case I would have thought you'd know me by now."

Still managing to keep myself in check, endeavouring to be a lot more business-like than the situation demanded and more polite than her tone deserved. "I'm wondering about that too madam. Could it be that I only tend to work on a Thursday, Friday, and every other weekend. Whereas today (being Tuesday), I happen to be filling in for a sick colleague, and our paths haven't crossed before?" Smiling all the while.

"What rubbish!" Adding, "I'm pretty sure it

would do your prospects no end of good if you were to learn the names of your most valued customers."

And I'm thinking that it would surely do her prospects no end of good, for being considered as a civil human being, if she wasn't being so bumptious. All the while sorely wishing I could get away with sharing my thoughts with her.

"Thank you, madam, that's very valuable advice, my apologies, but for me to help you I really need you to tell me your name?"

"Mrs Rebecca Trotman!"

Armed with her name I was now galvanised into action. Swiftly detaching the radio from my belt and still in close proximity to Mrs Rebecca Trotman, I put a call into the stockroom. "I have a Becky Troutman on the shop floor, can someone please bring her order through to the checkout."

"Do you mean Mrs Trotman Mike?" came the reply. "No, I'm pretty sure it's Troutman but you may well be right, let me check" …. As I looked across at Mrs Trotman who was clearly not amused, being even less so seeing me shrug and smile as I looked at her for confirmation. Anyway, her pre-paid order was brought out by Sharon, meaning that I was now relieved of duty. And without a thank you to any of us Mrs Rebecca Trotman left the shop.

Within minutes of her leaving the shop I received a message on the radio telling me that Gavin wanted a word. Then he appeared in all of his beige glory, gazing across at me from the threshold of the stockroom. My immediate reaction was one of surprise. I didn't even know that Gavin knew his way down to the shop floor. Without ceremony he beckoned me across with his index finger. "Michael, do you know a Mrs Trotman?" From the look on his face, I instantly knew that this wasn't one of his famed random questions. The other thing that occurred to me was his striking resemblance to a portrait I had once seen of Napoleon. Particularly his round head and small lipped mouth. Our Napoleon however had been stripped of his grand uniform. Being replaced with nondescript clothing made for an even shorter man. I also couldn't help feeling that he was still waiting for that one significant victory – in life.

"Yes I do know a Mrs Trotman as it happens, she was here about five minutes ago. If you hurry, she might still be in the carpark."

"She's just phoned in a complaint about you." As the only bloke on the shop floor my initial thought of asking for an identity parade to prove my innocence was going to be a waste of time, so decided instead to say nothing. Whether he thought that our ensuing silence might somehow cause me to break cover and offer an explanation, or even an apology, he was sadly mistaken. Because my attention was drawn to his spectacles slowly moving down his nose. Pushing his spectacles back with his index finger and bringing me out of my stupor. "According to Mrs Trotman, if she were you then she would seriously consider whether a future in retail was indeed the right career choice."

In that regard I would have to agree with her but didn't say as much. With Gavin's reprimand being received in the same uninteresting manner in which it was delivered, I thanked him for the advice, turned and went back to the till.

Our paths, mine, and dear old Mrs Rebecca Trotman's, were to cross once more which I'll share with you later.

* * *

For whatever reason the episode I've just been telling you about had an awakening effect on me. Not some epiphany, but an awareness that had been lurking just below the surface for some time, one which I'd chosen to ignore. And that awareness was how all of this, mine, and my colleague's lot, and how we were treated by many of our customers, had somehow become the accepted the norm. Until now that is.

Looking beyond The Country Produce Store there was no doubting that what we, my colleagues and I, were experiencing also had to be a daily reality for thousands of other people, working on shop floors right across the country. In other words what I was facing and being expected to tolerate wasn't only unique to me it had to be commonplace. This realisation humbled and agitated me in equal measure. Which I truly believe to be the catalyst for this book.

I was to subsequently speak with family, friends, and relative strangers all of whom were either working in or had worked in retail at some time or another, and my suspicions proved to be true. All were keen to share their experiences, much of which I have endeavoured to intertwine within this book, in some form or another.

FIFTEEN

WHERE MICHAEL TALKS FIRST AND THINKS LESS.

"Good morning, sir, I haven't seen you for a while, did you decide to retire after all then?" Said to a bloke that I hadn't seen in a while – obviously. Our chats would often centre around my retirement and his desire to do the same. Although apparently his wife needed some convincing.

Looking back at me for a moment he offered a solemn reply. "Kind of yeah, about a month ago I got laid off from my job and I haven't been able to get another one since."

This was one of a number of what I am choosing to call bloopers. Coming about as a result of having a loose tongue, connected to a scattered brain.

As you now know I was often the target for many of the rude sorts that came into the shop, frequently venting whatever happened to be on their narrow minds. But no more or no less than many of my colleagues.

However, I think it's time that I came clean. Whilst all of the anecdotes that you have now been privy to are based upon genuine real-life occurrences, I was also guilty of offending people, albeit (mostly) unconsciously, and thankfully very rarely. Or more to the point, opening my mouth without thinking. Although it must be said my misdemeanours were more of the blooper kind, rather than emulating the behaviours of the rude sorts you've been reading about. Let me give you some more examples.

I see a mature couple; I don't know probably in their late forty's early fifties – both had greying hair and a fair number of wrinkles if that helps – walking around the shop with twin babies in one of those ever-popular off-road strollers. Deciding to engage them in one of my passing the time-of-day kind of conversations. "What lovely babies, I'm looking forward to becoming a grandparent myself one day. You both look really happy? Although I'm guessing being able to give them back to their mum and dad at the end of the day is also nice too, right?"

It was the lady of the couple who responded. "We're not grandparents these are *our* twin boys."

Don't worry it gets worse.

At the till one afternoon a gentleman was waiting in the queue to checkout. He approaches my till and as I'm scanning his shopping he opens up a conversation. "I hope I've got everything on the list otherwise when I get home, I'll get such a hard time from my wife." Going on to tell me, "Last week I bought pork chipolatas instead of pork sausages and she gave me a right telling off, I don't know what all the fuss was about they tasted the same to me."

In a show of gender solidarity I offered. "Well maybe she ought to come and do the shopping for herself then sir!"

"She probably would if she could, but she's been bedridden these past four years."

One more and then I need to go bury my head in shame.

Walking behind a tall slim lady who was clearly looking for something specific. "Good morning, madam, is there something I can help you with?" The lady in question turned to face me, prompting me to change tack somewhat. "Good morning *sir*, is there something I can help you with?" Ultimately it was the goatee that gave it away.

SIXTEEN

WHEREIN A RARE STROKE OF (UNINTENTIONAL)
BRILLIANCE BY OUR LEADER. AND VICTORIA
SPONGE ADVICE IS GIVEN TO A MORON.

"I want three dozen eggs. And I know the sign says I can only have a maximum of one dozen because of the shortage. But who are you to tell me how many eggs I can buy?"

A very typical barrage from a very archetypal moron, that news reports of alleged product shortages in our shops, bring out.

One of several things I learnt during my brief time in retail was how much the news of a possible shortage of some commodity or other brings out the worst kind of moron. Not that any type of moron was a particularly welcome addition to my day, but as far as I'm concerned, these people can be categorised as the real crazies. During the COVID pandemic it was the alleged toilet tissue shortages, followed by car fuel which led to all manner of ridiculous behaviours. Despite news outlets, the same ones that ignited the panic in the first place, telling us that if we kept a cool head there would be enough for everyone. In spite of that, a considerable number of people still found it necessary to go out and collectively clear the shelves at their local supermarket or, in the case of fuel, run the garage dry.

But the thing is, news of a shortage does seem to be quite good for business. Once the story breaks, the shops can rely on the morons descending to mop up stock in just a few hours, which would ordinarily take days or even weeks to move on. The flip side is when something called supply and demand pricing starts to kick in. I'm not even going to try and explain the technicalities of how that works, because I'm not qualified. However, it would seem that when demand goes up then so do prices. Surely from a producer and sellers' perspective this must be pretty much the perfect storm. Though not necessarily for the shop floor worker.

Whilst store management are poring over spreadsheets, real-time sales data and sifting through holiday brochures, thinking how they will spend their bonuses, all from the safety of their high tower offices, shop floor workers are taking no end of flak from the morons that didn't make it to the store in time to clear the shelves. Likewise, although to a lesser extent, from the honest shopper who just wanted some tissue with which to wipe their bums. Or maybe have an egg for breakfast, which was the most recent shortage and one that I had first-hand experience of. Ranging from a tirade of questions about when the shop would get more stock in – and with any answer being unacceptable – to a variety of abuses. Particularly when trying to police the (shop managements) recommended amounts that people are being asked to buy at any one time.

Speaking to some shop floor workers from our local supermarket, they recalled instances where they had to either call security, or step in themselves to break up skirmishes between warring morons. In being told these tales I was encouraged to look online at the multiple videos showing people's behaviour. Particularly those that show them literally climbing over one another to get to some discounted goods, or some product or other that was deemed to be in short supply. In between many of these spats you will see the shop floor worker. The invisible victim of these crimes against decency.

* * *

In 2021, petrol stations across the land were imposing maximum limits on the amount of fuel car drivers could buy at any one time because of the fuel shortage, which was being linked to a lack of tanker drivers.

Our local garage, a small affair with only two pumps, set this limit to twenty pounds. Unless that is, you were a delivery driver or providing some other essential service – which didn't include grocery retail workers by the way. There were news items, both on TV and online, showing people getting up to all sorts of antics in order to get around these directives. Some clearly thought they were being clever – and then proudly posting their achievements on social media

– by putting the allocated amount of fuel in their car and then driving round to join the queue again (and again). Like I say, the worst kind of moron were on the loose. In the case of petrol stations, it would have been the petrol station attendant in the firing line as they faced the wrath of those people who demanded more than the company-imposed limits. And, of course, the price went up.

Where I live people pretty much behaved themselves. At our local garage there were queues from time to time, but we followed the rules, with signs telling us which way was in and which way to exit once we'd bought our allocated amount of fuel. Until that is someone thought that queuing wasn't for them and decided instead to drive up to one of the two petrol pumps by entering via the exit. The type of person – or two people as it happened – in question weren't the entitled sorts you've been reading about but a couple of fellas, way into their thirties I reckon, who still thought they were of an age where they could get away with wearing their baseball caps the wrong way round. Which I can only assume they believed made them look 'cool'. Whereas in reality they looked like a couple of ageing blokes who'd forgotten how to wear a hat properly. Having bullied their way to the pump, ignoring the looks and blaring horns of the rest of us, the driver leapt from their French hatchback and proceeded to give the rest of us a one finger salute with the one hand whilst lifting the petrol filling nozzle with the other. Our little corner of England was no longer an Area of Outstanding Natural Beauty – AONB – but an MOTL. And no not *My One True Love* or *Masters Of*

The Lightsabre, but *Morons On The Loose*.

However, the one flaw in their despicable plan was that before being able to put fuel into their car, the person in the little garage shop has to flick whatever switch they need to in order to activate the pump. We've all been there at one time or another, standing poised with the nozzle in the petrol tank waiting for the attendant to bring our pump to life. In this case the young lady in the garage shop just looked across shaking her head. And with a huge grin across her face as she stared down the now seething not so cool fella. This act of defiance also seemed to enrage the passenger in the French hatchback. Who in addition to his backward facing hat was also sporting a tee shirt with a faded ineligible logo on it. Which had clearly been washed a few times at the wrong temperature, evidenced by his exposed belly as he leapt, or rather unfolded himself, from the passenger side of the car. Expecting this coiled chunky slinky of an oaf to leap across the forecourt towards the little shop, I think we were all taken aback when he did absolutely nothing. He just stood there moving his gaze from his mate to the attendant, then us and finally back to his mate. All the while trying and failing to look menacing. Personally, it wasn't the gaze that I found particularly frightening it was his tee shirt progressively conceding the fight to contain his enormous girth.

This was clearly not going to plan, resulting in a standoff. By which time we had all gotten out of our cars, about six of us if I recall, and proceeded to do something very British. We applauded, specifically, the attendant in the garage shop. She in turn from her sitting position in the window gave us a theatrical bow. The (not so) young driver of the car, smelling defeat, slammed the filling nozzle back into its holster on the pump and clearly puzzled by our reaction merely fell back into his car without saying a word. The other fella, the one with the not so mean stare, decided to ungracefully withdraw by also getting back into the car. But not before sharing some philosophical words with us all. "You're all a bunch of fuckers!"

A small victory in the ongoing rebellion against morons I grant you, but I'm pleased to have been there.

* * *

With The Country Produce Store being on the periphery of mainstream grocery shopping the effects of the latest wave of panic buying went largely unnoticed. Although with supermarkets fast running out of, in this case eggs, the mob turned their attention elsewhere. We were hearing about the little shops on garage forecourts, like the one I've just been telling you about, being stripped of eggs and then moving on to the locally produced ones, occasionally on sale at the village post office counter, also being swallowed up.

Gavin was often slow to react to market forces, proven by the hundred or so toilet rolls sitting out back in the stockroom, with him having missed the last opportunity to cash in by at least ten days. In his defence though, according to some social media feeds there was still an alleged shortage at the time that he placed the large order with the wholesaler.

Once the wholesaler was flush with stock (see what I did there?) our order arrived at Goods In on multiple wooden pallets. We were then enthusiastically instructed, by a jubilant Gavin, to make space for these rare treasures on the shop floor. But nowhere near any door because of potential 'grab and run opportunists.' This, by the way, was a Gavin term, undoubtedly made up in the moment. Sadly, for him his get rich quick, retire tomorrow plan on the back of toilet roll sales were scuppered almost immediately. Because the supermarkets, who had probably used the same wholesaler, also started to receive their deliveries. And let's be honest few people would look to The Country Produce Store, or any farm shop for that matter, for toilet tissue. Even if it is organic, and hand rolled by a local toilet paper artisan, on the thigh of a free-range donkey.

As local social media went into meltdown with people asking where they were going to get their next egg from, Gavin instructed the marketing department – his wife – to put a notice online something along the lines of; *'The Country Produce Store asks you to please be considerate to other customers by only taking the number of eggs that you absolutely need'*. A rare stroke of pure (unintentional) brilliance by our leader. At the push of a button the world not only knew that eggs were still available but where they could be found. *#thecountryproducestore*. But even better than that, because the word on the street was that there were no limits being imposed at The Country Produce Store, just a naïve 'please be considerate' request. I'm sure music to the ears of a particular type of selfish moron. Thinking to themselves, from the comfort of some soft furnishings made from double quilted toilet rolls; 'be considerate?' 'Good luck with that mate, those rules don't apply to us.' At the same time putting word out on their moron messaging group. "Get your arses across to The Country Produce Store. They've got eggs!"

Another notice I stumbled upon, whilst perusing 'Friends of The Country Produce Store', social media page. The backstory was this: A customer was trying, and had been for some weeks, to arrange a funeral reception (or wake) for a terminally ill friend. She put out a 'save the day' notice due to the need to coordinate caterers and so on. The plan was to hold the event in a marquee on one of the fields adjacent to the farm shop.

Robert (Bob) Cuttings funeral reception – update. Event Postponed - Please do not attend as Bob has made a full recovery.

The heightened activity on social media strongly suggested that the genie was well and truly out of the bottle. In turn Gavin let those of us on the shop floor know, via Angela the Shop Floor Manager, what had gone down, leaving us to prepare for a likely onslaught as he retreated to the safety of his office to watch events unfold on the one CCTV camera that worked.

So, there we were – poised. For what we didn't really know, because people coming to our shop en-masse wasn't something we'd had any previous experience of. The most that we'd ever had to contend with, even at Christmas, arguably our busiest time, could best be described as an occasional flurry (of people) I guess. Should we control entry? Does anyone amongst us have riot control experience? Should we switch the lights off and pretend there's no one here? Just a few of the thoughts and questions being posed. As it turned out it took the crazies a little time to organise themselves, because that initial day, following the posting of our egg advice note, went off pretty much the same as any other one. Apart from the frayed nerves that is.

However, the next morning driving in at a quarter past seven, the carpark seemed unusually busy. There were even one or two people hovering around the entrance, despite us not opening for another fifteen minutes.

I was assigned to the checkout so oblivious to the rush at opening time as people came in, clambering for eggs. Within minutes the first of them started to make their way to the till, bypassing the butchery counter on the way. "Can I interest you in some bacon to go with those eggs?" enquired Gary, no doubt seeing an opportunity.

One smart arse customer fired back. "Is there a shortage of bacon then?"

"There could be mate if you buy a lot of it."

But no, few if any were interested in adding bacon or anything else to their baskets, on that ridiculous morning. But a good effort on Gary's part though. So up to the checkout they came and no I wasn't going to let them off the hook.

First up was a man and his partner with arms full, managing to carry four boxes of half dozen eggs each. Greeting them with my best patronising smile. "Looks like someone's planning to do a lot of home baking, am I right?"

Clearly wanting to pay for their booty and get out of the shop as fast as possible, perhaps to rush home to get their eggs on to some online marketplace or other, meant they were not up for conversation. But I wasn't going to be rushed. Neither was I going to miss an opportunity to engage with the moron fraternity. Call it research if you like. So, keeping it at the level of small talk. "Sorry, I was just curious as to why so many eggs. It's just that we do get a lot more home bakers in the shop these days, especially since the COVID lockdowns." They were having none of it, and I'm sure I even detected a tiny bit of embarrassment on their faces. Although unlikely as you'll find few if any of these types of people are gifted with anything resembling principles or humility.

Time to up the ante – despite the ever-increasing queue. "Do you have a favourite cake? I know I do, my wife's signature cake, a Victoria sponge, which, unless I'm mistaken takes about four eggs I believe. Just think you could make six Victoria sponges – each!" Clearly small talk or any talk for that matter, wasn't the order of their day and so running out of steam I just finished off by asking whether they would like a carrier bag – or trolley – to make it easier for them to carry their eggs to their car. Even responding to that simplest of questions seemed too much for them. So, I took their money and let them leave in peace.

Do you work here? – The shop floor chronicles

One bloke was upfront and told me, before I could hit him with any of my inane conversation, how he had no real plans for his eggs purchase but planned on freezing most of them. To which I simply nodded and took his money. I could have further explored what his method was going to be, I guess. Only because I remember reading somewhere that eggs can be frozen but there are certain things you have to do with them first. Such as removing them from their shell. However, I had a strong feeling that many of those panic bought eggs weren't destined for the freezer, the mixing bowl or foodbank. And as much as they (eggs) do have a relatively long shelf life, I suspect that many of them would have ended up in landfill. Though long after they had made an appearance on social media that is, probably a selfie – eggs with their proud owners, besties forever! Or at least until the recommended 'use by date'.

Others came and went without further molestation from me as I quickly came to realise that few if any panic buyers have much in the way of any depth of character. I am also confident that they are unable to explain to the rest of the sane world why they insist on behaving as they do.

The good news is that The Country Produce Store shifted most of its stock of eggs resulting in the local producer being able to afford to take a short holiday. After the initial rush things seemed to calm down a bit. Although with Christmas on the horizon I was fully expecting an announcement on the news that poultry will be in short supply. Probably from some Turkey farmer. As it turned out I wasn't to be disappointed, because soon after the shop started to do its initial planning for Christmas, the newspapers and news stations were awash with Christmas turkey shortage stories. And you know what? Every person that wanted a Christmas turkey from us that year still managed to buy one.

* * *

Quick leap forward to February 2023 and there was an announced shortage of salad goods in the UK due to something or other happening in Spain. Long story short, and as I explained to the Spanish plum lady people, we seem to have gotten used to having all manner of foods all year round so when such things are not available it, of course, makes the news headlines. Personally, I tend not to be an all-year round salad eater – or anytime of the year salad eater given the choice – despite my wife's best efforts to the contrary. Anyway, here's a little gem for you – if you know your lettuces, you will know what I did there.

Walking the shop floor one morning Sharon saw a woman kneeling. Thinking she'd slipped or had some kind of turn she rushed over to assist. Only to find the lady in question taking a selfie kneeling next to the cucumber display! Each to their own of course. But what did occur to me when I was told the story; is that when this salad shortage becomes a distant memory in say a few weeks' time, I wonder what people will be thinking when they stumble across this picture of a woman looking very pleased with herself kneeling next to a large quantity of cucumbers? I'd like to think that the classic Ken Dodd punchline will once again be evoked. And most definitely not

Sharon's, "… I think I need to take that and do something with it."

SEVENTEEN

DARK CLOUDS, PAKAMACS AND VIOLENT AGITATION
COME TO MICHAEL'S LITTLE CORNER OF ENGLAND.

"Stop thief!"

Shoplifting, a scourge of the shop floor and
something that undoubtedly goes on in shops across
the world. So, I shouldn't have been surprised when
it turned up in my little corner of England. As far as
my retail experiences go this was as far from the
many humorous ones I'd had and worse than
anything the belligerents could throw at me.

Our daughter and the many other retail people
I've spoken with all agree that it's a problem that
shops have never really found a solution to – and it's
getting worse. And not just a problem for shops but
for them personally.

Accordingly, a shoplifter is not someone that fits
a particular profile or mould. In other words, they
come in all shapes and sizes. Old, young, in-between,

wealthy looking, not so wealthy looking, smart, scruffy, amateur, professional, I'm sure you get the picture. And most often it is the shop floor worker that we find on the front line (again) when shoplifting occurs. Particularly troubling when it turns violent, as it often does. The British Retail Consortium website is full of tales from shop workers who have been subjected to all manner of both physical and verbal abuse at the hands of shoplifters. Commentators and politicians periodically raise it as something that needs to be clamped down on. However, rarely do those words turn into credible solutions.

Closer to home our daughter and her colleagues have so many stories to tell of shoplifters and how they have a genuine fear when they witness someone stealing from the shop. Even though they are told not to engage a shoplifter, but to simply raise an alarm, they are nonetheless often targeted simply because they've been seen doing just that. One went on to tell me that if he sees someone lifting something and heading for the door, he simply turns his back. Such is his fear of being seen, in his words. "Of dobbing someone in." Added to that the very real prospect of being set upon as he makes his way to his car at the end of the day.

Having been on the shop floor when an item was lifted and then watching helplessly as the young perpetrator made for the exit and into a waiting car, I decided to do some research on the subject. Specifically, how I might spot a shoplifter. I found some advice online from Police.UK that focused specifically on behaviours. I played this back to my colleagues, and whilst they agree that much of what the website says is true and they are often able to spot a shoplifter a mile off, there are so many that just do not fit a described profile.

During my time on the shop floor there were numerous occurrences of shoplifting. Some were blatant and others acting suspiciously very much along the lines of the behaviours described by Police.UK. But most acted no differently from that of the regular shoppers. For example, one such lady, neatly turned out and later discovered to be well spoken, decided that since she had come into the shop the weather had taken a turn for the worse, and she therefore needed one of our pakamacs or fold away bagged mackintosh's as they are referred to today.

If you are old like me, you might remember these from your childhood. Dead popular in the 1950's and for a few decades thereafter, and for some inexplicable reason, making a comeback. They come in a variety of colours ranging from sensible black to bright gaudy ones. However even with the introduction of these striking colours the wearer still looks a bit of a numpty. Moreover, that look, brings with it both wanted and unwanted attention for its wearer. So, in shoplifting a pakamac, in the way that our lady was doing, meant that it was unlikely to go unnoticed.

Having taken it from its little bag, which she thoughtfully put back onto the display unit, she proceeded to put it on, button it up and pull the hood up, all the while looking at herself in the provided full length mirror. Being pleased with the fit, although maybe not the look, she subsequently decided that she would take it – literally – without paying. As she proceeding to exit the building, she casually waved at me. "Excuse me madam you need to stop please!" Whilst simultaneously alerting anyone on the airwaves to the fact that we have a pakamac heist in progress.

"Sorry Mike can you repeat that please, are you wanting a pakamac price?" Followed by a chuckle. But Maureen was on it in a flash, as she materialised out of nowhere as a superhero might. Though thank goodness she didn't feel the need to arrive wearing her lady pants on the outside of trousers.

Long story short – the lady in question, after a few minutes of insisting to Maureen that she *had* paid for the coat, left the shop. But not before taking the garment off and throwing it onto the floor. In doing so assuring us, in no uncertain terms; that she will never shop at The Country Produce Store again. And will most certainly be telling her friends about the treatment she had received. But this was a lightweight encounter compared to the many stories I've heard and ever thankful that my personal experience of shoplifting was nothing by comparison.

As we got nearer to Christmas there's no doubt that shoplifting became more prevalent. Sadly, few were caught, and although one or two did become quite aggressive I'm pleased to say that there was only one incident that ended in some sort of direct confrontation.

A group of about three came in and displayed some very obvious behaviours suggesting that they probably weren't there to shop. Proceeding to grab a couple of bottles of rum from the alcohol section they raced through the exit and into a waiting car. Unfortunately for them, in their haste to get away the door of the car wasn't closed properly, and it hit one of the many concrete posts bordering the carpark. Furthermore, one of the inhabitants' coats fell out of the same door resulting in the car having to stop to allow a gang member to get out and retrieve it. By which time I was outside the shop and watching their getaway, when the young man who'd gotten out of the car saw me. He smiled and before getting back into the car gave me the ever popular two finger salute. I in turn smiled and gave him a one index finger salute pointing up at the CCTV camera a few feet above my head.

"We received a call about some shoplifters, can we speak with a manager please?" Blocking the light to my checkout stood a well-fed gentleman police constable and a slightly older, less well-fed lady community support officer. Both humourless.

Enter my smile. "If you're here about the most recent incident, then I'm sorry to say that you've missed the perpetrators by about forty-eight hours. But thanks for coming anyway." No reaction and still humourless. So, I lifted the radio from my belt. "Gavin, the police are here for you." That should shake him up a bit.

To all you shoplifters out there. If you happen to be reading this book, and whether you bought it or stole it I don't care, but the next time you feel the urge to go steal from a shop have a thought for the people working there. Leave them alone. It's not their fault they are just doing their job.

EIGHTEEN

ILLUSTRATIVE OF THE MODERN ERA WHERE A JOLLY
HOLLY AND ALL HALLOWS TIME OF THE YEAR ARE
BEDFELLOWS ON THE SHOP FLOOR. WITH A COMING
TOGETHER OF THE CONVIVIAL AND THE MIRTHLESS.

"We're having our granny for Christmas dinner."
Announced an excitable little boy.

"How lovely for you. We're having turkey." I
replied.

I'm a Christmas lover – always have been.
Consequently, when Christmas conversations were
occurring out the back of the shop, I was getting
genuinely excited. Okay it was only September but
why not? Within days of those initial whisperings
Gavin and his entourage (otherwise known to the rest
of us as the creeping chaos) were pacing around the
shop floor. Pointing at nothing in particular and
gesticulating where certain Christmas displays were
to go. Elaine was summoned from behind the deli

and Pete from the butchery counter to give their thoughts on how their counters might complement the overall look of the shop. Other discussions included where they could hide Halloween.

Halloween, unlike in the US, has never been a big deal in the UK. We have got better at it mind you, and children today seem to look forward to doing a bit of trick or treating come the day. But as I say nothing like the US, where you see whole families throwing themselves into it and wearing costumes that would not look out of place on a film set. Whereas the British children haven't really progressed much beyond the old white bed sheet over the head, for that classic ghost look. The Country Produce Store was very much in the same vein. Although being a particular type of shop they were of course expected to sell pumpkins – organic. Despite few of them ever being eaten. In doing so and with some reluctance they decided that it might also be expected of them to sell a few witches hats, scary masks, and the like. So, when Christmas started to pick up a pace, Halloween, which was still a few weeks away, was relegated to a place nearer to the stockroom and well off the beaten track. People, looking to buy a pumpkin, would often come up to the till and ask if we had any Halloween things. At which point they'd be directed to a single shelf some way off beyond the artificial Christmas trees. As for trick or treat sweets that was a definite no no. Don't get me wrong we did sell sweets and chocolates but I'm thinking that an after-dinner mint, honey covered seed bar or chocolate covered pork rind – yep there is such a thing – would be considered more of a trick than a treat.

As always, the little coffee shop endeavoured to step up to the occasion, in this case by offering a Halloween ghostly latte. From what I could tell the only difference between that, and a normal latte was the addition of a marshmallow skewered onto a wooden stick and placed precariously across the top of the cup. I decided to ask one of the Ali's what was particularly ghostly about any of it, regretting doing so almost immediately. "Surely even *you* can see how a marshmallow resembles a ghost. Especially if you stretch it a bit."

"To be honest no I can't, maybe it would help if you drew a face or something on it. The marshmallow that is, to give it a bit of individual character – no?"

"We don't have the time for that, just use your imagination – if you have one."

But some people did seem to get it, especially those whose children insisted that they wanted a ghostly latte. In spite of many of the younger ones not actually liking coffee. In doing so they were also prepared to pay the extra twenty pence.

Over the next few weeks of September, The Country Produce Store was transformed into a Christmas wonderland. Tables and display units, that I'd never seen before, were brought from an offsite storeroom, and shoehorned onto the shop floor. Christmas produce was being delivered almost daily, ranging from food stuffs to locally sourced, locally designed, made in China, Christmas adornments and decorations.

Do you work here? – The shop floor chronicles

Though the early seasonal excitement wasn't for everyone. During this Christmas autumn time people would often come up to the checkout shaking their heads. "Christmas already? Surely not, it's too early for Christmas," and so on. In return I would often tell them that the only reason we were putting the Christmas stuff out now is to make room out in the stockroom for the Easter eggs. This would sometimes get a laugh, although more often an incredulous look and another shake of the head. To make matters worse, or better, I would offer my usual farewell, with a bit of festive cheer thrown in for good measure. "You have a pleasant day and a Happy Christmas!" Although, on that last point, I was advised by my colleagues not to peak too early.

As we turned the corner into November, with pumpkins now way past their best and reluctantly reduced in price, Christmas was really picking up a pace. Decorations were flying off the shelf as indeed were the seasonal food stuffs. The types of things that people only seem to buy at Christmas. Such as dates, Christmas chutneys – because they've got some spice in them that people associate with Christmas – liquor infused fruit cakes, mince pies, special Christmas sweets, chocolates galore and a whole lot more besides.

Some though needed to be sold quickly as the best before dates were often weeks before Christmas day. And of course, we sold the whole range of nuts. Walnuts, Brazil nuts, almonds, hazelnuts… all still in their shell. For us Brits cracking open and eating these types of nuts seems to be one of those unique Christmas rituals. As we set about them with a pair of nutcrackers (we sold those as well), often pinching fingers in the process. But even so, the threat of severe injury does nothing to deter us from entertaining the notion of getting a nut out of a shell with these fourth century B.C. designed implements.

The nut decides, at your first feeble attempt, that it has no intention of being cracked open. But then after you apply, what is no more than a miniscule amount of additional pressure, it changes its mind and gives way entirely – catching you and your fingers completely unawares. But in spite of the pain you are triumphant, ignoring the disproportionate amount of effort you've had to exert, for a nut and a blood blister. In our house, as I am sure is the case in houses across the Country, a bowl of nuts will sit on the sideboard, hardly touched, well into the new year, until they are finally disposed of, and the bowl put away until next Christmas.

Some of the other food stuffs that I noticed people buying just for Christmas, although many are available at most other times of the year, include: flavoured cheeses, mulled wine, gherkins, other pickles and chutneys, Brussel sprouts, turkey, glazed hams, tinned chocolates and toffees, bread sauce, Port, Sherry – I'm sure you get the picture, and maybe do the same. I know we do. Although I've noticed, particularly at Christmas, that when a ribbon is tied around say a jar of chutney or there's a printed picture of a robin on a packet of biscuits the price rockets. But people seem oblivious. Me included. I'm a sucker for a tin with a robin on the lid. You only have to look in my shed at most of my nail and screw containers.

Do you work here? – The shop floor chronicles

According to management, by the end of November pre orders for Christmas meats and deli produce were at record levels since we came out of the COVID lockdown. Nothing, it would seem was going to spoil Christmas this particular year, with calories being considered as no more than the number that it is. Not even the customers, who were becoming increasingly rude as the pressure cooker, that is Christmas, started to boil, could spoil the optimistic mood that was building throughout The Country Produce Store. Though nothing could have prepared me for the unseen intolerable torment. One that was to send me to the edge of madness – Christmas music.

Don't get me wrong I love a Christmas tune and over the festive season I'm told by my family that my kitchen karaoke is second only to that of a caterwauling cat – allegedly. But those same songs, the ones that I have cherished for decades, became the songs of the devil. They were played repeatedly all day, every day, so much so that I couldn't get them out of my head. It felt as though they were being absorbed into my very being. By the end of each day, having heard those same tunes for the previous six weeks, day in day out, murder was very much on my mind. Especially if someone dared to come up to the till whistling along to whatever Christmas song happened to be playing at the time.

* * *

Christmas food orders were in high demand with the system for people to order stuff being as simple as it could be. You (the customer) fill out a form and pay a deposit. We (the shop floor person) give you a copy of the form with the deposit receipt stapled to it. You (the customer) bring said form back into the shop on the date that you have stated you would like to collect your order. Whereupon your order will be waiting for you. "So, tell me, how is it that so many people get into such a tailspin over this simplest of systems?" I found myself asking this very question to Sharon one morning.

"I've no idea, but that's people for you."

"I'm not sure that's helping."

"That's all I have."

* * *

"I've come to collect my Christmas order."

By December the thick skin I had developed over the previous months meant I was now impervious to some people's lack of grace or manners when they spoke to us. Even so I still managed to extend a smile to even the most unworthy. "Certainly sir, do you have the customer copy of your order form with you?"

The gentleman in question is now looking confused. "My wife never mentioned any order form, she just asked me to pop in and collect our Christmas order."

"Sorry sir, but it would be really helpful if you have your copy of the order form, otherwise we have no way of knowing who you are and what you've ordered."

"It's Tremlett and I know my wife would have ordered, amongst other things, pork sausage meat because I asked her to – if that helps."

No of course it didn't help. Was he a Tremlett or has his wife ordered a Tremlett? I don't understand! I didn't want to understand, I just wanted him to bugger off. These ruminations were becoming increasingly frequent. Perhaps I needed to see a shrink to get some *Retail Therapy*. Or maybe I needed to pull this bloke across the counter by his ears. Coincidentally 'God rest you merry gentlemen' was playing across the store. Oh God where are you when I need you, I'm thinking. Because here was a gentleman, standing in front of me, that I'm pretty sure could have done with a rest – a really long one.

And relax. "That's not helping sir, perhaps you could phone your wife and ask?" I was assuming he had a phone of course, but I check anyway. "You do have a mobile phone don't you sir?"

"Yes of course I have a mobile phone, what sort of person do you take me for?"

I'm hoping that's a rhetorical question.

About 15 minutes later, having found the only corner of our carpark where you can get a phone signal, he came back in. "She doesn't know anything about a form either. She says she wasn't given one. And the name's Tremlett in case you've forgotten."

No not forgotten, just hoping you'd forgotten your way back into the shop.

"But we give all of our customers… Never mind. I tell you what sir if you could stand to one side for a moment so that I can serve this other customer. Then I'll see if we can sort this out for you."

"Will you be long?"

"Who knows? [shrugging] This checking out business doesn't seem to be an exact science you know." The waiting customer, to whom I now turn to, smiles as I proceed to scan his groceries. As he leaves, he wishes me the best of luck but diplomatically avoids wishing me a Happy Christmas.

Turning back to the Tremlett. "Can your wife remember what she ordered sir?"

"Yes of course! Sausage meat, which I've already told you about, a joint of meat, which may be lamb but could equally be beef, definitely not turkey as we're not keen on turkey, some cheese, and a large pork pie."

Detaching the radio from my belt I call anyone on the airwaves for help at the checkout. I then explain to the approaching Sharon that I'm just off to the butchers to see if we can somehow hunt down Mister Tremlett's order. "Hasn't he got his copy of the order form then?"

"No and remind me to smack you when I get back." I then turn to Mister Tremlett and ask him to stay where he is, as I head off towards the butchers.

Some ten minutes or so later Gary manages to retrieve the order for Mrs Tremlett, going on to tell me that according to the form it isn't due to be collected until Christmas Eve and today's only the fifth of December. I didn't even respond I just accepted the proffered photocopy of the form, which he had kindly done for me, and headed back to Mister (halfwit) Tremlett.

Do you work here? – The shop floor chronicles

"Mr Tremlett! The good news is that we found your order and here's another copy for you. Try not to lose it. The not so good news is that your wife's requested collection date is Christmas Eve, so therefore your order, particularly the leg of lamb and other fresh goods, haven't been delivered to us yet and won't be for at least a couple of weeks."

"Yes, I know my wife told me all that when I spoke to her earlier. It's just that I was in the area, and she thought it would be a good idea if I popped in and collected our order. I'll have to leave it for today then I suppose. She will be disappointed mind you, my wife that is, as we were hoping to have the pork pie for our tea. Never mind, see you on Christmas Eve I guess."

Don't you fucking dare wish me a Happy Christmas!

Of course, he didn't wish me a happy Christmas nor thank me in any way whatsoever. He just left the shop no doubt to lose the copy of the Christmas order form I had just given him.

* * *

Over in the coffee shop everything was looking nice. They had their own music running throughout the day, a CD of some church choir or other – on repeat. This meant that if you stood on the threshold between the shop and the coffee shop it was like listening to two Christmas radio stations both of which were slightly off tune.

Both the Ali's were wearing playful red Christmas hats and Ben, who was on his school (college) holidays, a fetching little elvish hat.

Footfall was also increasing as curious people came in to sample the Christmas coffee ranges. Nothing very complicated mind you, just adding some gingerbread or cinnamon syrup to many of the existing classics. Although, like our ribbon clad jars of chutney, this added extravagance provided an excuse for a disproportionate increase in price.

This was also the season for hot chocolate, now available with gingerbread or cinnamon syrup, and being offered in various sizes. There was the standard cup of hot chocolate for the unadventurous. Going on up to the whipped triple choc with squirty cream and mini marshmallows on the top extravaganza – for those with a proper sweet tooth. The other addition, if you enjoy a sprinkle of chocolate powder on your latte or cappuccino, were the Christmas stencils. The Ali's were especially proud of these, and customers seemed genuinely excited at the prospect of being taken through the whole pantomime of choosing which shape they'd like to see on top of their coffee. The little plastic stencils were available in multiple shapes, including a smiley face, a panda, a snowflake, a Father Christmas hat, a Christmas tree, and a whole range of others that weren't particularly Christmassy. Even people waiting in the queue got involved, having an opinion on what should or shouldn't be selected. And then seemingly holding their breath as the chocolate powder was sprinkled over the stencil, followed by a theatrical reveal of the chosen shape. On a couple of occasions, I'm sure I even heard a gasp. There was one problem, however. Inasmuch as there was a seasonal beverage price hike the length of time it now took to serve each customer meant that sales actually fell over the Christmas period. The other thing was, that after a (very) short period of time – because certain stencils were more popular than others – the plastic started to deteriorate.

So it was, that on one of our days off Elaine and I decided to go for a morning coffee at The Country Produce Store coffee shop. And in doing so savour the customer experience of having a festive shape adorn our coffee. For our cappuccinos I chose a snowflake and Elaine a Father Christmas hat shape.

Even before the coffees arrived Ben was apologising for the stencilling, which I assumed to be a reference to his skill, or lack of skill, in the art of chocolate powder sprinkling. As he gently placed our coffees down onto our table he continued to apologise, telling us that new stencils were on order. I remember waving him away and telling him not to worry, adding that I'm sure I could not have done any better. Until that is, I looked down at my cup, expecting to see a chocolate snowflake, only to find myself gazing upon a perfectly formed swastika. Elaine put her hand over her mouth, both in shock and to stifle a laugh, until she looked down at her Father Christmas hat stencil, which had also seen better days, only to discover a chocolate powder penis gazing back at her from the top of her cappuccino. We both looked across at Ben who from the relative safety of now being behind the counter, simply shrugged and turned to nervously ask another unsuspecting customer what stencil they would like on their latte.

* * *

Notwithstanding a few curious out of towners, the clientele remained pretty much the same as the rest of the year. The only notable difference being the coffee morning mums – The Thicket.

As it was now officially holidaying time they would appear with broods of both pre-school and school age children. Having already experienced the pre-schoolers nobody was surprised to see that the school age children were equally as obnoxious, but over the years had perfected their craft into becoming downright hideous and with minimal manners. Although on a positive note they weren't as rowdy as their younger siblings, due in no small part to their complete lack of social interaction, largely brought about by them being wholly focused on their smartphones. Not that this is unusual of course in these modern times. I find that it's now commonplace to see whole families out for a meal, or in this case a coffee, and each member, parents included, staring at their phones. Completely ignoring one another. I also regularly see parents pushing a stroller with the one hand whilst holding and looking into their smartphone with the other. One time I even witnessed a toddler, of no more than two years, being pushed around the shop by his or her mother, holding a small tablet device. Whilst mum, in between picking stuff off the shelves, was wholly engrossed in messaging on her phone, or whatever else it is busy mums do these days. The point I'm making is that there was no interaction between mother and child.

They of course all wanted, and were given, the biggest of anything on the menu. Such as the whipped triple choc with squirty cream and mini marshmallows on the top of hot chocolate. Accompanied by large slices of cake, just in case they needed a bit more of a sugar rush. Upon seeing this their younger siblings insisted on the same. But give their mums their due they didn't take any nonsense from these pint-sized bullies, oh no. Once again, I would be witness to one or other of The Thicket laying down the law. "Of course you can have it, so long as you finish it all up." And did they (finish it all up)? Well let's just say that most of what was ordered for their brood ended up on the floor, the table, in pushchairs and in the food bin – as opposed to their darlings' little mouths. One other notable addition to this group, as we got nearer to Christmas, was the coffee morning dads. Sorry, I don't have a collective noun for them. Having also finished for Christmas they'd accompany their brood for a morning coffee and a dose of chaos. However, after just a few minutes it would become increasingly obvious to the casual spectator, that the novelty of spending time with their family was already wearing thin. To think that they still had the whole of Christmas to get through. Arguments around the shop were now commonplace, often ending with the coffee morning dad opting to go wait in the car. In other words, excusing themselves from the chore of shopping and having any association with his own children. But what the coffee morning mums lack in the smarts department they seem to make up for with cunning. Because I would often see coffee morning dads leaving the shop with all the children in tow. After all, this according to one conversation I happen to overhear. "The children really want to spend some time with you darling, because they don't get the chance very often as you're so busy working so very hard for us all." Nice!

* * *

Back on the shop floor Christmas Eve was upon us in no time at all, so a shorter but extra busy day ahead. Although let me take you back to the day before.

"Excuse me, are you busy?"

Number two or three in the list of stupid question, but not necessarily the most ridiculous I'd had to field. That would be a toss-up between A). "Are these avocados local?" or B). "Are you open?" To give B some context – it was mid-morning on a Saturday and the shop was heaving with customers.

"Busy? of course not sir, how can I help?"

"That's great. Well, I have a problem and that is that my fridge is broken and I'm due to collect my Christmas order today."

"So, is it that you'd like to delay the collection of your order until tomorrow sir? Because I'm sure it wouldn't be a problem." See how helpful I can be when I put my mind to it.

"That's very kind of you, but I was wondering whether I could pick it up on Christmas day?"

Here we go! "The problem is sir that we're closed on Christmas day so I'm not seeing how that can work. But I tell you what let me reach out to a

manager and see if we can come up with something."
I was on fire.

So, I radioed to Angela (our inconspicuous shop floor manager) for assistance. She uncharacteristically arrived promptly, and I went through the gentleman's predicament with her before she took control of the situation. "But we're closed on Christmas day."

Always good to have a manager in the know. "I know. I've already explained that to the gentleman." Nodding towards the fellow in case she hadn't yet realised who he was.

At which point, and I kid you not, the gentleman in question added. "That's inconvenient, you being closed on Christmas day, I mean. Is there any way at all that someone could let me into the building just so I can collect my order?"

With retail experience coursing through her DNA the thought of grabbing the gent by the lapels and launching him out of the shop didn't seem to cross her mind. Me on the other hand?

In case you didn't know - *There are multiple definitions of the acronym DNA. There is the one that most commonly springs to mind – Deoxyribonucleic acid – the genetic information carrying molecule. But there are multiple others, such as - Does Not Apply, Do Not Ask, Do Not Answer, Definitely Not Attractive ....* And too many others to name. And no, I'm not going to tell you which one I'm using in the case of Angela.

Angela on the other hand, and give her plenty of due, she still endeavoured to find a solution. "Let me see if one of the owners, who live quite near, can help you out." She then proceeded to get on the radio to Gavin to see whether he would ask the relevant question to the owners. However, that conversation never made it past first base. And no, not because Gavin is incapable of asking a relevant question, he knew that the owners were already away skiing and will be for the duration. Turning to the gentleman to give him the bad news. "You probably overheard that; the owners are away so I'm sorry it looks like we won't be able to help you after all. Although you can leave the collection of your order to last thing tomorrow if that helps, we'll be closing at three on Christmas Eve".

"No that won't do at all! I was hoping I wouldn't have to go buy a new fridge until the boxing day sales. But seeing as you're unwilling to help, I guess I have no choice do I? Anyway, you'll have to keep my order until tomorrow now as I've got to spend the rest of today to go buy a fridge!" And so turned tail to leave the shop. Angela in turn scuttled back to the relative safety of her little office and I got on with my life – almost.

"Sorry sir but you can't go out that way, that's the entrance." I could have overridden the auto sliding door switch to let him out, but I had used up my daily ration of 'goodwill to all men' at about the time he announced that we weren't willing to help him.

"But the exits at the other end of the shop, can't you open it for me?" He (almost) pleaded.

Yes of course I could. "No sorry sir I can't it's against the rules." At which point I left him to fume a little more, and to maybe reflect on his behaviour, as I turned to get on with some random job at the furthest point from him and the entrance.

The thing I love about rules is that they can sometimes come in very handy. I disagree that they are made to be broken. But should, at all times, be considered as optional.

NINETEEN

MICHAEL LEARNS THAT GOODWILL TOWARD MEN IS
RARELY EXTENDED TO SHOP FLOOR WORKERS AT
THIS FESTIVE TIME OF LOVE.

"Reality is merely an illusion, albeit a very persistent one." – Albert Einstein. Referring to the passage of time as an illusion and that time, like space, has no direction.

I would never dare to challenge one of the smartest people ever born. But I do wonder how he might have felt about that particular piece of wisdom had he worked on a shop floor at Christmas time. Where the *reality* is the experience of the shop floor worker. And the *illusion* being the Spirit of Christmas, Seasons Greetings, Peace on Earth and my personal favourite, Christmas is for spreading love and joy to everyone around you. Cynical? Maybe. Honest? Definitely.

Do you work here? – The shop floor chronicles

In our house Christmas wouldn't be Christmas without a Quiz. With that in mind you might like to have a go at the shop floor Christmas quiz.

To make things easier for you, all the questions are real life situations that cropped up on or around the Christmas period. You'll find the answers at the end of the quiz, although there's no prize on offer – other than my hearty thanks to you for buying this book. Unless you are a shoplifter of course.

See how you go – Good Luck!

Question 1 – A shop floor worker is walking up the aisle with a stockroom trolley laden with fresh fruit and vegetables – Do you?

a) Let them know that they are in your way.

b) Stand your ground and get them to manoeuvre around you.

c) Step to one side to let them pass.

Question 2 – A shop floor worker tells you that one of your Christmas shopping items is out of stock until the day after tomorrow. But they can phone you when it comes in – Do you?

a) Ask to speak to a manager.

b) Tell the shop floor worker that it just isn't good enough and social media will know about this.

c) Tell the shop floor worker that it is inconvenient, but yes please a phone call, to let them know that it's in, would be great.

Question 3 – You open a packet of biscuits in order to keep your child quiet. After eating a few the child decides that they don't like them – Do you?

a) Leave them somewhere on the shop floor.

b) Leave the shop with your child and the packet of open biscuits without paying for them. And proceed to drop them in the nearest bin.

c) Tell the person on the checkout what happened and offer to pay for them even though you don't want them.

Question 4 – It's Christmas Eve and a shop worker breaks the news to you that we're out of bread sauce, and in doing so apologises profusely – Do you?

a) Insist that the shop floor worker phone around local supermarkets to ask whether they have any.

b) Tell the shop floor worker that they've spoiled your Christmas and then put your shopping basket full of shopping on the floor and leave the shop.

c) Be annoyed although accepting of what you're being told and wish the shop floor worker a Happy Christmas.

Question 5 – During a particularly busy time just before Christmas the tills go down. In other words, they stop functioning until the system is reset – You are told that they should all be back online in less than 5 minutes – Do you?

a) Create a collective stir with others in the queue. Telling them all that; "This just isn't good enough!"

b) Shout at the shop floor worker on the till to hurry up because. "I'm in a hurry!"

c) Let the shop floor worker know that you understand that these things happen and then wait patiently for things to come back on.

Question 6 – You see an item that has either fallen or has been nudged from a shelf – Do you?

a) Walk around the item pretending not to see it.

b) Drive you trolley over it and although it gets caught in the wheels still do nothing.

c) Pick it up and place it back on the shelf.

Question 7 – A shop floor worker has very obviously priced up an item incorrectly. A slip of the price gun means that a £10 item is priced at £1 – Do you?

a) Rush to the till with as many of the items as you can carry before the error is discovered. Even though you probably don't want them all.

b) Phone your friends to; "Get down here quickly."

c) Bring it to a shop floor workers attention because the error is such that whoever priced it incorrectly is likely to get into a lot of trouble.

Question 8 – An item's 'Best Before' date is todays date – Do you?

a) Rant at the shop floor worker that the shop is trying to poison you.

b) Hold the item really close to the shop floor workers face in case they haven't seen the date clearly.

c) Advise the nearest shop floor worker that you've noticed an item's Best Before date is today.

Question 9 – A shop floor worker is wearing a Santa style Christmas hat – Do you?

a) Tell the shop floor worker that it is not Christmas for everyone and therefore wearing such a hat is inappropriate.

b) Tell the shop floor worker that wearing such a thing isn't in keeping with the reputation of a high-end shop.

c) Wish the shop floor worker a Happy Christmas.

Question 10 – You drop a particularly expensive Christmas Panettone on the floor. The box breaks open and its contents spill onto the ground – Do you?

a) Put the now empty box back on the shelf and kick the Panettone under a nearby table.

b) Blame the Panettone box for being difficult to handle and walk away.

c) Let the nearest shop floor worker know so that they can clear the mess up.

Bonus Question 11 – You see a Big Issue vendor outside the shop selling the Christmas edition of the Big Issue and in doing so wishing passers by a Happy Christmas – Do you?

a) Ignore them completely by either looking the other way and or avoiding eye contact.

b) Tell the vendor that you don't have any change despite the vendor telling you that they can now accept card payments.

c) Ask them to step aside so you can pass.

d) Be rude in some other way.

e) Offer a Christmas greeting and possibly buy the Big Issue.

Answers: There are no correct answers just those that your conscience says ought to be the right ones. However for questions 1 to 10 – Choices A) & B) in each case are unfortunately actual responses that either my colleagues, my retails friends or indeed myself, received from customers over the course of the festive season. Answer C) was a rare thing indeed.

For the bonus question 11 – Answers A) through to D) are regrettably the most common responses. However, there were a few E)'s – Happy Christmas and a prosperous new Year to you few.

Michael Ethelson

TWENTY

NAVIGATING THE GAP BETWEEN CHRISTMAS AND
THE NEW YEAR. WHERE CUSTOMER EXPECTATIONS
REMAIN UNCHANGED, AND THE BANANAS ARE TIRED.

"I can't believe that you're not open on New Years Day. That is so inconvenient. I really don't like the idea of spending my holiday shopping for food before I actually need it."

The time of goodwill toward men, if indeed there was such a time at The Country Produce Store, has definitely come to an end.

Back to work a few days before the end of the year, but only open for a limited number of hours each day. So short shifts. Although customer expectations remained largely unchanged as their attention shifts from Christmas festivities to New Years celebrations. All of which I found quite interesting. Not the change in attention from one event to the other, but the fact that customer expectations remained largely unchanged. It didn't seem to occur to some people, as they came into the shop looking to buy fresh produce and other similar foodstuffs, that factory workers, food producers, packers and the like were also enjoying a well-earned rest. Although the year was just about to end on a high for me.

"Good morning, sir," said an intelligent looking young man, one half of a youngish couple. The fact that they started with a good morning and a 'sir' to boot, and didn't ask if I was busy, or whether I worked here, resulted in them having my immediate and full attention.

"Good morning to you both, how can I help?"

It was now the young lady that took over proceedings. "My parents are over from France for the New Year, and we'd like to give them a traditional French New Year's Eve experience, make them feel at home, that type of thing. I have a shopping list of things we'd like." And with that she handed me the list.

Ordinarily, as you now know, I tend not to volunteer myself up as a personal shopper. It isn't that I don't want to help – most of the time – it's mainly because I'm really busy – all of the time. However, as we had started off on the right foot I broke with personal tradition and took the proffered list from the lady, and read each item back to them, to make sure that I got everything right. "Okay, so what do we have here? Foie Gras (or other French Pâté), oysters, lobster or crab, snails, champagne, large baguette (times four), French cheese (an assortment) and ingredients for pancakes".

I looked up at the pair and was just about to speak when the young lady, maybe detecting the air of uncertainty I was giving off, smiled at me. "I know we're probably pushing our luck a bit with the snails and oysters but hopefully we're good for the other things."

I smiled back to them both and looked down at the list once again to compose myself. Before starting from the top, and progressively working through it. "Foie Gras, I'm sorry but we don't have any of that although we do have a selection of pâté, but I can't guarantee that it'll be French. Same for the lobster or crab I'm afraid, in that we don't have any and in fact rarely do. Snails and oysters as you'd already guessed, champagne, again no, but we do have some sparkling wine from a local vineyard, which I've been told is very good although quite expensive." All said with as much encouragement as I could muster.

Looking up momentarily to gauge the mood, I continued. "Large baguettes, also no, sorry, although had you come in earlier you may have been lucky. The good news is that we do have some French Brie on the delicatessen, and we have all of the ingredients in the shop to make pancakes." I'm trying to remain positive and sympathise in equal measure, but surely, they didn't really expect to come into an English farm shop and buy such specific food for a French dinner party – did they? All of which I kept very much to myself.

I looked from one to the other, seeing the young lady particularly crestfallen – clearly, they had. I handed the list back and in doing so apologised. Not because The Country Produce Store had somehow let them down but because I didn't know what else to say.

The young man took the list, thanked me for my time, and as they turned, I heard her whisper. "What are we going to do now?" Obviously she had set her sights on doing something a bit special for her mum and dad, so I felt compelled to try and offer an alternative solution.

"Excuse me but can I make a suggestion?" Going on without waiting for permission and in doing so directing my attention at the young lady. "If as you say, your mum and dad are living in France, do you think it would be nice for them to come over and maybe have a traditional *English* New Year with you both? Something which of course they wouldn't get over there."

I'm sure I could hear the cogs whirring as they looked at one another and contemplated my idea. Then the young lady smiled at the young man who in turn smiled back. So, this is what love looks like I'm thinking. They then nod at one another, and both turn, now directing their smiles at me. "We agree, that's a great idea!" the young man said, looking at his partner for final reassurance before proceeding. "What do you recommend?"

I thought about this for a few seconds and then confidently offered back. "I have absolutely no idea." And continued to smile having given them the answer they most definitely didn't want to hear. However, before I completely spoiled their day. "But

I know someone who probably will have an idea, just give me a moment," and with that I got on the radio and asked if Maureen could come out onto the shop floor. Which she duly did in full rollerblade style. After I had explained everything to her, she was spurred into action, taking the young couple away and around the shop giving them all manner of ideas as they went.

Job done and being a little bit pleased with myself at the outcome, I carried on checking the bananas, which since Christmas Eve had turned from being proud phalluses to limp ones, most of which were sporting very bruised skins. As I was separating the good from the not so good, I recalled Ross's wise banana evaluation words. "If any of them look like they have a serious STD then gently remove any of the really infected ones from the bunch and put them to one side. But don't pull them, gently tease them away from the others." I remember thinking at the time, but not for too long, in what world did Ross live in where he'd experienced an STD that looked like a rotting banana?

For context and the unenlightened. *STD – Sexually Transmitted Disease. Not – Short Term Disability or Spot The Difference or Screw The Dealer or any number of the other 90+ uses of the STD acronym.*

And so it was, as I was gently teasing with some infected bananas the aforementioned young couple came up to me, with a basket full of who knows what, and proceeded to wish me a Happy New Year. Now that is what I call a result, if ever there was one, in this shitty, wonderful job on the shop floor.

Followed within minutes by a fully paid-up member of the 'Entitled Brigade (Ladies Division)'. "Excuse me but I can't seem to find any strawberries, and I need strawberries for a pavlova I'm making for a new year's gathering." And as an afterthought. "You aren't busy, are you?"

Normal service has resumed. "No madam I'm not so busy. Unfortunately, we sold out of strawberries over Christmas, and we probably won't get a delivery now until early into the New Year."

"But I need strawberries for a pavlova......" I reflected that it's been almost a year since my very first contact. Some things, I'm referring mostly to the people, never change.

* * *

As we turned the corner into the new year the principal focus was to offload as much of the Christmas stuff as quickly as possible, before the 'Best before' and 'Use by' dates caught up with us. In other words, all or anything with a festive flavour was to be marked down in price, with most being moved to a designated place in the shop. Asking management if we should leave the Christmas display tables out for the Easter eggs, I was encouraged not to be so stupid – Apparently we were still months away from Easter.

Even with the considerable number of yellow reduction labels, adorning many of our product lines, which on any other day would have people climbing over one another, there was still a noticeable drop in footfall. I guess due to the fact that most people's next pay day was still some way off towards the end of January. We were most definitely at that time of the year where people tightened their belts waiting for the cost of Christmas to hit home. I know because that's how it has been in our house for years.

Customers that did cross our threshold during those early days of the new year, were mostly regulars. Many of whom I recall telling me how they were relishing the prospect of Christmas and having all the family joining them for the duration. Most were now visibly exhausted. With quite a few revealing. "Thank God that's over." Which for moral support I wholeheartedly agreed with. Although not referring to the time with my family, as I can never get enough of that. As I laugh along with them and watch them trudge out of the door, I'm pretty sure they will be back again next year. Full of enthusiasm for the coming festive season and looking forward to once again having their families descend on them.

It was also time to take down Christmas decorations and give the place a thorough clean. Over the course of first couple of weeks of January all the tins, bottles jars and so on were progressively taken off the shelves. Each item was given a decent dusting and put back again – labels facing forward. The other thing that the lull gave us time to do was a complete stock check. Arguably the dullest job ever, and one that gave rise to quite a few arguments and re-counts, as shelf quantities varied considerably with what the stock system was telling management.

Coming home one evening I shared my day with our daughter who works for a very large retail concern. Only to be told that many of the things that I was experiencing in our stock check weren't dissimilar to how it was at her place. Bearing in mind that her retailer employs super amounts of technology. I'm not sure if I felt better or not. All I know is that there would be more of the same the following day and my back really ached.

In fact, I was tired on quite a few levels and once again marvel and take my hat off to all the retail heroes out there who somehow manage to work on the shop floor for years on end. Turning up day in day out, night in night out, smiling (most of the time) and seeing to the needs of their customers. Often as though each one, at that moment, was the most important thing in their life. A look that I was never able to master. Which of course they are I guess, because customers are vital for the livelihood of the shop they work in, so therefore by extension vital for their own livelihood. But on the other side of coin, we must also acknowledge the shop floor workers resilience. No matter how many times they are knocked back by the types of belligerent characters that have been referred to throughout this book, they keep getting right back up again.

With the downturn in customers came the downturn in available hours. My zero hours contract gave me no minimum hours guarantee and so it was, almost inevitably, that my hours were cut. Which to be honest I didn't have too much of a problem with as it meant that others, more reliant on securing a decent number of hours, wouldn't be impacted and I could give my back a rest.

TWENTY – ONE

A MELANCHOLIC WIND BLOWS AS MICHAEL BOWS
OUT. BUT STILL TIME FOR A FINAL REPRISE WITH
REPRESENTATIVES OF THE ENTITLED BRIGADE.

"Do you have any ambitions Mike or is this just a job for you?" Another day, another round the table lunchtime conversation with a few of my young colleagues.

"Absolutely! I quite like the idea of working in a DOC shop."

"Is that a charity shop?"

"Nope, a shop Devoid Of Customers."

I continued to turn up when called upon and do what I hoped was a decent job for The Country Produce Store. But instinctively I knew that my time in retail was coming to an end. I had discussed it with Elaine over the Christmas break and agreed that once we had gotten through January, I would hand my notice in. My retail experience had run its course, and my continued backache now needed a permanent remedy. Although I have to say that despite everything, and in so many ways, this had been such a worthwhile adventure. And so it was, just a few days after my decision to depart, that I had perhaps my last noteworthy engagement with not one, not two but three of the 'Entitled' brigade.

* * *

The first significant delivery of fruit and vegetables had arrived in the shop early one morning in the first week of January. Up until this point we only had sporadic deliveries comprising of a small selection of staples such as potatoes, carrots and so on.

Keen to get them out and on to the shop floor I was tasked with coming in early to get stuck in – stripping out the existing produce and replacing it all with fresh. Less a quality check and more a complete overhaul. Meaning that little thought was given over to the usual practise of reducing the price or wasting off old produce. Those decisions would have to wait until later. So, I had two trolleys on the shop floor – one laden with new fruit and veg and another, which wasn't so laden, with the old stuff. Ordinarily I would have taken the latter trolley back out and into the stockroom, so as not to clutter the shop floor, as well as to avoid unwanted attention which I'd had once before. However, on this occasion either as a result of being focused on getting the new stuff out, or an attack of stupidity, I really don't know, because the unwanted attention wasted no time in descending upon me.

Do you work here? – The shop floor chronicles

Head down making sure my display of long-stemmed broccoli looked as though it had actually grown out of the wooden display box – as opposed to looking like it had been thrown at the box – I was alerted to voices coming from the trolley of old produce whose future had yet to be decided upon. I looked up and saw an elderly gent and two elderly ladies sifting through a small pile of savoy cabbages, as though they were at some jumble sale going through second hand clothes. In doing so ignoring the fact that much of the produce was falling from the trolley and on to the floor.

I Rarely missed an opportunity to encourage people back into line these days. "Excuse me, please can I ask what it is you think you're doing? Those items are not for sale right now, but if you give me a few minutes, I'll have all the fresh vegetables and fruit out on display that *will* be for sale. In fact, if it's a cabbage you're after I have some on my trolley right here – pointing to the fully laden trolley of new produce – which you're welcome to choose from." Within the spirit of keeping the customer onside and not wanting to engage with them any more than necessary, I chose to ignore the fact that their rummaging had spilled much of the old stuff on the floor. So opted instead to give them the best smile that I could muster, so early in the year.

Disregarding everything I had just said the old gent took a half step forward. "I'm sorry but you looked busy, and we didn't want to disturb. But now I have your attention can I ask what's wrong with these cabbages, because they look alright to me?" Without waiting for an answer, he went on. "Are you going to throw them out? Because if you are, I'd be happy to take the whole lot off your hands – for nothing of course." He then turned and winked, let me say that again in case you missed it, he turned and winked at the elderly ladies. Clearly on a mission to impress his two mature doxies, and at my expense it would seem.

Standing up so as to avoid him literally looking down on me, keeping my smile intact, but equally wanting to move them along. "The future of all the old fruit and vegetables on that trolley, including the items that are now on the floor – sorry I couldn't help myself – has yet to be decided upon, which happens to be my next job, once I've finished putting all this stuff – once again pointing to the trolley laden with new produce – out on display." Thinking that this brief encounter had been dealt with I proceeded to kneel back down to continue to neatly bunch my broccoli.

Although they weren't done yet. "But what about these carrots and onions, what are you going to do with these?" I looked up and saw him holding aloft a handful of carrots whilst one of his lady friends a couple of onions, one in each hand. "They'd make a wonderful vegetable soup you know. Can't we just take them?" And with that he started to place the items into one of our brown paper bags, whilst giving me some advice as to how he might blag some free veg. "Look if you write on the bag the word 'free' I can explain as much when I get to the checkout. I wouldn't want to be accused of shoplifting for the sake of an onion, or two." Going on to make a strange nasal snickering sound which I took to be a laugh of sorts.

I had to give him full marks for persistence despite his increasingly irritating manner and ridiculous snickering. To be honest with you I wasn't so aggravated by him trying to grab himself and his little harem some free ingredients to make soup. No, it was his supercilious manner that was really getting under my skin. In his world I had the distinct feeling that he was the clever sod and the rest of us existed on a much lower level. I had come across these 'types' of people hundreds of times in my life and had grown to dislike them intensely.

However, I really did need to close this down and as he looked like he wasn't going to budge, I decided to swallow my pride and offer, what I thought, was a decent compromise. Therefore, stopping what I was doing once again, and with some other customers now taking an interest in the unfolding drama, I offered to go through whatever vegetables they had their eyes on. "I tell you what, let me go through the vegetables that you think you'd like from *that* trolley. Any that *I* decide are not fit for consumption we can ignore and any others I can let you have for say half price. How does that sound?" Looking around at the one or two bystanders I noted nods of approval at my reasonable stance, undoubtedly knowing I was dealing with a particularly odd situation.

"But who's to say whether something isn't fit for consumption?" Said the other lady friend, who up until that point had been somewhat in the background.

"That would be me madam, as I've just

explained." And then without further ado I started to go through the old cabbages offering up a couple that I thought to be in reasonably good condition.

"But what about the others, why can't we have those for nothing?" Said the persistent gent.

Momentarily detaching myself from this unfolding piece of nonsense, I began to wonder what the repercussions would be for beating someone within an inch of their life with a rotten cabbage.

Anyhow, with an air of authority for which I had no right to have. "I'm sorry no, they smell wrong. And as they say [I had no idea who 'they' were] 'if in doubt throw them out', and I'd have serious concerns about selling you those cabbages. At the end of the day if you were to develop a stomach-ache as a result of eating a dodgy cabbage then it's our reputation, and my job, that'll come under the microscope. So, no I'm sorry you can't have anything that I deem to be unsuitable."

"Well, there's no need to take that attitude we thought we were doing you a favour by taking some old vegetables off your hands."

Yes of course you did.

It was now my turn to ignore everything being said to me, including further protestations from the gent that he was prepared to take the risk. In silence I proceeded to apply the same logic to some onions and carrots. I then bagged them up, put a half price note on the bag and offered the whole lot to the gang of three, which they ungratefully took.

Seeking to avoid any further contact, and not

affording any one of the audience the same opportunity, I bid them all a good day, picked up the discarded vegetables from the floor, put them back on the trolley, and marched the whole lot out to the stockroom. Promptly returning to my safe place a few minutes later – my fruit and vegetable display bubble. Although you know what they say about bubbles. It only takes one prick to burst them.

Within minutes however I was to be interrupted again, this time by another fella, clearly in a hurry. "Are you going to be long, it's just that I need some courgettes and I see that you haven't got them out yet?"

I wearily looked up at the man. "Soon sir, very soon."

Regarding the three old sorts I of course received no thanks for my trouble but did get some unwelcome free advice from the old gent, as they exited the shop. "If you don't ask you don't get you know." He was right of course, and I was counting the days to my leaving The Country Produce Store – before I did something that could be used against me in a court of law.

* * *

Three months later and I'm back in The Country Produce Store, this time as a customer. My trip to the local supermarket failed to provide a decent joint of meat for our Sunday roast, so I thought I would splash out and get us something locally farmed. It also gave me an opportunity to meet up with old work mates and have a chat with my wife, who was and still is, queen of cheese on the deli. Old habits die hard I guess because as I was walking to the tills from the butchery counter, I noticed a couple of bruised granny smith apples. Without a second thought I picked them out and handed them to yet another new shop lad, who I had been introduced to just before I left, on what turned out to be my last shift. It was as I handed the two apples over that a deep condescending voice from my not-too-distant past called across to me. Getting louder, as I turned, instantly recognising its owner striding towards me.

"Excuse me, you there, I've come to collect my order. Six dozen eggs, in boxes of six, four organic spelt loaves, two litres of organic semi skimmed milk, in one litre cartons, three large pork pies and a small carton of double cream. Oh, and six plain scones." Before I could explain that I no longer worked at the store, she moved in and peered at me, as though looking at some specimen or other under a magnifying glass. "I know you, you're the fellow who couldn't remember my name."

Not in any mood to engage with, or antagonise, the delightful Mrs Rebecca Trotman (remember her?) I simply told her that I did remember her, and her name of course. Going on to tell her that I no longer worked at The Country Produce Store. "I decided that retail wasn't the right career choice for me after all." In doing so folding back the months and giving her my best smile.

No doubt sensing a note of sarcasm in my voice, she simply turned to the new lad, gave him a withering look, and barked the same collection order that she had just reeled off to me. He in turn eagerly responded. "No problem at all madam, can I have your name please?"

"Oh, surely you must know who I am! are you new here? I'm pretty sure it would do your prospects no end of good if you were to learn the names of your most valued customer's young man." Ouch!

Time for me to leave the building I reckon – for good.

The Country Produce Store prayer.

You fathers (and mothers), who art in our shop (hopefully with your extended family)

Hallowed be your name (on your debit / credit card)

Our customers come,

who will be done (in so many ways)

on the deli as much as on the butchery.

Give you this day our artisan bread

and forgive us our price hikes,

as we forgive those who pish against us.

And lead us not into discounts.

But deliver us from shoplifters.

For this is our kingdom,

The organic fruit and the vegetables,

Forever and ever

Seven days a week.

Amen

EPILOGUE

It has now been quite a while since I left the employ of The Country Produce Store. And yes we did get the planning permission we were after. Consequently I'm back on the tools doing what my body fights against me doing – everyday. So I still have backache (and knee ache, and neck ache…) but on my terms. Is this the last time that I'll venture back into the workplace? Well you'll have to wait for Chronicles 2. Because Elaine tells me that The Country Produce Store are likely to be short-handed for Christmas. I'm also being asked to go back into the corporate world to act as some kind of mentor for a bunch of up and coming bright young things.

The not so good news is that I miss the camaraderie of the shop floor. Occasionally going back as a customer, I still share a joke or two with the likes of Sharon, Maureen, the Ali's, Fran, and the lads on the butchery. But the dynamic has of course changed. I'm no longer part of that inner circle – or the inner rectum as Fran calls it – and therefore cannot really claim to empathise with what is going on in their daily lives, despite my previous experience. Whilst it is true that many of the challenges they shared with me are similar to what they always were, there are so many other contributory factors that go to make up each and every daily experience. I no longer have that appreciation.

I am sure there are quite a few more anecdotes, dramas and characters out there just waiting for an audience. For example, 'whistling man,' could have got a mention. This by all accounts is quite a common affectation and for some reason seems to be the sole tendency of middle to old age blokes. For some inexplicable reason these blokes find it necessary to walk around shops and whistle – tunelessly – continuously. Often with their hands behind their backs as though they are out for a stroll in the park. Or how about those that seem astonished by the idea of having to pay for their shopping. As random whistling seems to be men of a certain age, then this peculiarity is very much in the realm of the ladies – though age doesn't seem to be factor in this case. "How are you paying today madam?" Often receives a look that says, "I haven't really thought about that bit." Followed by a frantic rummaging in the bottom of whatever bag they happen to be carrying for their purse.

Then there are those that get openly annoyed, often taking their frustration out on some poor shop floor worker, because the shop management or company management have decided to make some changes (improvements) around the place. I'm referring to the, "This is ridiculous, moving things around. I can't find anything anymore," brigade. Within The Country Produce Store, we often suffered as a result of new ideas and theories from the management team. Always taking care not to put into practice anything they suggested.

Lastly, I could have maybe told you about the parents that deposit their kids in the shopping trolley despite signs telling them not to do so. Or maybe those people that drape themselves over their trolley, using it as some kind of mobility aid, as they move around the shop. I don't know why this irritates me, but it does. Maybe because it just looks so slothful, and my upbringing didn't see being slothful as something you advertise to the world. Particularly by hanging over the handles of a shopping trolley.

There were many other silly 'for sale' ads. For example, the little girl who asked me to compose a postcard for her because she was looking for a budgie cage for her gran. I know what you may be thinking, but don't worry I couldn't do that to such a polite little girl. So, the wording I composed for her left people in no doubt that the little girl was on the lookout for a cage, with which to put a budgie into, and not her gran. One that I didn't edit though:

For sale – household and garden items. Double antique metal bed, with mattress. And two old sleepers.

One of the main drivers in publishing these chronicles, apart from my own experiences, was as a result of listening to the views, insights, and anecdotes of quite a few shop floor heroes. Often followed up with the phrases such as, "You couldn't make it up" or "Someone ought to write a book about this," or my personal favourite "Someone ought to put this place into a theatre at Christmas, it'd make a great pantomime". As I was unable to strike a deal with a theatre this book will have to do.

My time on the shop floor has been a life changing experience never to be forgotten.

My co-workers, the customers (love them or not), the often-ridiculous situations that I used to find myself in, all contributed to something that was truly transformative. To the point where I now have a significantly more-heightened awareness of just how much we, the general public, ought to be grateful for the service and dedication of these often invisible and unloved heroes – our shop floor workers. In my opinion – the forgotten essential service.

Even today, and beyond The Country Produce Store I still find myself reacting to behaviours.

During a visit to our local supermarket I see a man knocking a packet of breakfast cereal from the shelf and on to the floor, with his trolley. He then proceeded to kick it to one side and walk on. Seeing this took me back to my time on the shop floor, and how I had both been a witness and remediator of such behaviour. In a past life, I probably would have turned a blind eye to this act of indecency. But not anymore.

Will, by making an obvious point of picking it up and placing it back on the shelf, lead to a change in this man's future behaviours? Obviously, there's no real way of knowing, but I have to hope. I also live in the hope that someone won't punch me on the nose, as I continue on my one-man crusade against the blight that is bad manners, particularly in shops.

As much as my own awareness has been heightened by the briefest of sojourns into the world of grocery retail, I sincerely hope that this book will, in some small way, heighten the general public's consciousness of just how important these people are to our daily lives. In doing so it is further hoped that it will have a positive impact, by shining a light on the poor attitudes and behaviours of quite a few people out there. And who knows it may even go some way in changing them. Although in reality I suspect that many of the types of people I have described throughout this book, are too long in the tooth, or indeed have no idea just how dreadful they really are. But I remain optimistic.

As for you good shoppers out there – just stay as you are. Who knows some of how you behave may rub off on the others. Thank you for reading this book. And if you're thinking about going shopping anytime soon – be nice!

Michael Ethelson

BEFORE YOU GO

Supermarkets are the biggest single employer in the UK.

The wholesale and retail trade are the most dominant employment sector in the UK.

2022 – Union of Shop, Distributive and Allied Workers (USDAW) annual survey of a proportion of retail staff relating to levels of verbal abuse, threats, and assaults.

- 74.26% have experienced verbal abuse.
- 49.25% were threatened by a customer.
- Nearly 8% were physically assaulted.
- 40.88% said violence, threats and abuse caused them anxiety at work.
- 29.97% are now considering changing job.

And the numbers go up year on year.

Do you work here? – The shop floor chronicles

A report published by the British government - Violence and Abuse Towards Retail Workers, (2021), provides detailed insight into the extent of what I consider to be a national disgrace. Additionally, this report, and any associated reaction to it, never made the popular national news headlines. There was some reference to it in the preceding month, but you would be hard pushed to find it. Interestingly, or perhaps just a sign of our times, on the day that it was published the country focused on England football and the Euros, Princess Diana's old Ford Escort being sold at an auction and a whole bunch of what I consider to be less newsworthy other stuff.

When the real news was this: *"The last 5 years has seen a shocking rise in attacks on retail workers. The Association of Convenience Stores (ACS) found that 89% of individuals working in local shops had experienced some form of abuse. The British Retail Consortium reported that the number of incidents recorded last year amounts to the equivalent of one a minute during a typical shopping day. The appalling truth is that for millions of shop workers verbal abuse and physical violence is becoming a too frequent reality…"*

The report went on to say that: *"Shop workers are the lifeblood of local high streets and communities. During the height of the COVID-19 pandemic those in essential retail continued to work and kept our communities going."*

I ask you, where in a caring world would the following statistics (also contained within the same report) not have made news headlines?

"...the equivalent of over 50 (physical violence and abuse) incidents an hour or almost one a minute during a typical 9-hour shopping day also including an average of 11 violent incidents every hour or roughly one every 5 to 6 minutes."

More recently The British Retail Consortium (BRC), published its BRC CRIME SURVEY 2023. Sadly there were few surprises but nonetheless this is what it revealed.

- *BRC survey shows high levels of retail violence and abuse, at over 850 incidents per day.*
- *Retail colleagues are being physically assaulted and threatened with weapons.*
- *Nearly a billion (£) lost to customer theft, with eight million incidents in 2021/22*

...incidents, including racial and sexual abuse, physical assault, and threats with weapons, rose from the pre-COVID high of over 450 per day in 2019/20, to over 850 per day in 2021/22.

I can't help thinking that if these statistics were for, say, professional footballers, or actors, or other celebrities they would have been splashed all over the airwaves, on social media and in our newspapers.

So, with all that in mind, I have one final question for you:

Why is it that so many people find it necessary to

behave with such enmity towards shop floor workers, and conduct themselves so reprehensively? You may well have done so yourself in either some small way or in a more serious way; I'll just leave that question hanging.

For further information check out the **BRC CRIME SURVEY 2023 at brc.org.uk**

And finally – I promise.

Continuing on the subject of invisible salespeople, I would like us to give a shout out to the Big Issue vendor. Most often to be found on or around our high streets up and down the country. And outside in all weathers. For my money one of the toughest sales jobs anywhere; taking cold calling to a whole new level. And what do most people do? I'll tell you – although you probably already know. These vendors are more often ignored, despite their best efforts at civility, sometimes even verbally abused. I have yet to come across a Big Issue vendor that doesn't offer a pleasant greeting, a: "Good morning," or a "Good afternoon,". So, whether you want to buy what is being offered or not – although I would urge you to give it a go because it's actually a good read – at least have the courtesy to positively engage with the person. Respect the fact that like millions of you, they are also getting out of bed each day and going off to do a job. They most certainly do not qualify for the nuisance-burden that many people consider them to be.

Happy Shopping!

-Ends-

ABOUT THE AUTHOR

Micheal Ethelson is just a bloke who tends to see the world through a non-tinted lens – in other words seeing the world for what it is. He will never understand nor is he accepting of how bad manners, rudeness and other inconsiderate behaviours have somehow become normal in our society. His focus though isn't on those popular more newsworthy injustices – so you won't find him glueing himself to motorways or tying himself to trees to make a point. Instead he has chosen to use the pen to get his message across, hopefully raising an awareness of those people who, for some reason or other, find themselves without a voice – such as our shop floor workers.

Printed in Great Britain
by Amazon

53697277R00146